WHO'S YOUR DADDY?

Life Lessons from
the Prodigal Son

WHO'S YOUR DADDY?

Life Lessons from the Prodigal Son

WHO'S YOUR DADDY?

Life Lessons from the Prodigal Son

Copyright © 2006

Scripture quotations marked NIV are from THE HOLY BIBLE, New International Version, copyright ©1973, 1978, 1984 by The International Bible Society. Used by Permission.

Scripture quotations marked GNT are from the THE HOLY BIBLE, Good News Translation - Second Edition © 1992 by American Bible Society. Used by permission.

Scripture quotations marked NRSV are from the THE HOLY BIBLE, New Revised Standard Version of the Bible, copyright © 1989, by the Division of Christian Education of the National Council of Churches in the U.S.A. Used by permission. All rights reserved.

Unmarked Scripture quotations or quotations marked KJV are from THE HOLY BIBLE, King James Version, public domain, or are the author's paraphrase.

Paperback:

    ISBN 10: 0-9785572-0-4

    ISBN 13: 978-0-9785572-0-1

Digital Edition:

    ISBN 978-0-9785572-7-0

Printed in the United States of America
10 9 8 7 6 5 4 3 2

SIMMONS
PRESS

Simmons College of Kentucky Inc.
1000 South 4th Street
Louisville, Kentucky 40203

Acknowledgments

I would like to thank the loyal, dedicated, hard-working men and women of the most wonderful church in the world—the St. Stephen Baptist Church in Louisville, Kentucky. These persons give far above and beyond what is required of them. They, along with the faithful and competent faculty and staff of Simmons College of Kentucky, are playing a vital role in shifting our paradigms of understanding regarding ministry. Surely through their service, future generations may know that ministry extends far beyond the pulpit and even beyond the walls of the church itself.

Table of Contents

Preface

The nearly four decades that I have served as pastor of St. Stephen Baptist Church in Louisville have been filled with spiritual adventures, challenges, and joys. However, in 2005 as I began the task of serving as the thirteenth president of Simmons College of Kentucky Inc. (formerly Simmons Bible College), I was reminded of the great responsibility that has been placed upon our shoulders to secure the future of our people. At one time, Simmons University was a preeminent institution of higher learning for African Americans in the state of Kentucky and throughout the South. Simmons University trained many of our doctors, lawyers, architects, and preachers. Simmons had a football team and a baseball team. They played against historic Fisk University, West Virginia State, and even beat Tennessee State in football. It was the only Black-owned institution in the country that had a law school, a medical school, and a seminary.

Standing on the foundation that was laid by our forebears, St. Stephen Baptist Church and Simmons College of Kentucky are growing. Back in the day, Blacks kept their institutions going with their meager earnings as domestics and laborers, both skilled and unskilled. They kept the school and the church going with fundraisers like the Sisterhood Tea they held in the St. Stephen B.J. Miller Educational Building. Various choirs and soloists came and sang an A and B selection. They would sing and leave their contributions of support.

In those days, they took a little and did a lot with it, like the 21-year-old Madison County, Kentucky student who always made sure that he sat at the front of his class at Simmons so that he could learn to read and write. That was in 1922. Our people were only one generation removed from slavery, and many Blacks still couldn't read or write. He and others came to Simmons to learn to read and write because they had a great hunger for education. That young man was not only the first pastor of St. Stephen Baptist Church; he also was my grandfather, B.J. Miller, Sr.

Even though our colleges, universities, and seminaries are now integrated, we still need institutions like Simmons. We still need institutions of higher learning that, within a cultural context, train preachers, teachers, missionaries and ministers, and also prepare people for life so they can get a good education. I have embarked upon this journey with certainty that we, the thousands and thousands of Baptists across this region, can maintain one college. That is the vision, and we have been doing it!

God has given me a vision for the school, and part of that vision is Simmons College of Kentucky Press, which will provide a publishing venue for our faculty and others in the region, as well as generating additional income for the college. With a great deal of effort, ferocious energy, faith and prayers, Simmons College of Kentucky has held and will again assume a prominent role in higher education in Kentuckiana and the surrounding region. We have made incredible progress, as we now enroll over 200 students and offer five curricular areas: religion and theology, business (entrepreneurship), communications, music, and sociology. These areas specifically support the five pillars that undergird Black institutions: the church, business, arts, media, and family. In time, as we continue to grow, we will continue to broaden our offerings.

It's important for us to continue telling our story of how we got over. Tell your story and keep it alive. A song is not a song if you don't sing it, and a bell is not a bell if you don't ring it. A story can't be a story if you don't tell it. And by the grace of the Almighty, we will continue to train our leaders for the future and to tell our story through Simmons College of Kentucky Press.

Kevin W. Cosby, D. Min.

Foreword

Relationships are perhaps the most important reality in the human experience. Our relationships with other human beings and our relationship with the One who made human beings determine our perspective on life, our ability to function, our aspirations, and our ultimate destination.

This principle is taught biblically in both the Old and New Testaments. This principle is also taught in African culture, which predates the writing of the Hebrew Bible. In the Old Testament the Prophet Micah (6:8) says, *"He has told you, O mortal, what is good; and what does the Lord require of you but to do justice, and to love kindness, and to walk humbly with your God?"* (NRSV).

To do justice means our relationships with others must be just. How we treat those whom Jesus calls "the least of these" determines whether or not we are in a just relationship with them and whether or not we are justified with God.

To love mercy implies relationship. We who have received mercy are to be merciful in our dealings with others. Our relationships with others must be seasoned with the sacred condiment of mercy.

To walk humbly with our God is the foundational principle for life in this world and in the world to come, and that principle is based upon our relationship with God. For Micah to call Him *"your*

God" and for us to embrace the words of the psalmist, "For this God is *our* God even unto death," means that we are in a relationship with God. Our relationship with God is a given before we are even aware of it. God gives us life, and God gives us God's breath, binding us in relationship to God from the day we are born until the day our breath is called back to God.

The book of Genesis teaches us that it is not until God breathes into our nostrils the breath of life that we become living souls. We have no life apart from the breath of God. Our relationship with God is inextricable.

God makes us in God's image. In the words of Dr. John W. Kinney, dean of the Samuel DeWitt Proctor School of Theology at Virginia Union University, God "donates some divinity to dust", releasing God's Self into our care in order for us to be fully human. The quality of our life depends on our relationship with God. Either we cultivate that relationship for the good, or we neglect it to our detriment.

In the New Testament when questioned by the Pharisees as to which is the greatest commandment, Jesus replies by quoting and modifying the book of Leviticus: "Thou shall love the Lord thy God with all thy heart, with all our soul, with all thy strength and with all thy *mind*!" The passage Jesus extracts from Leviticus does not have the word "mind" in it. The Son of God adds to the sacred Scriptures from the first Testament to underscore the importance of basing our relationship with God on being made in God's image.

When Jesus quotes the word "love" from the Old Testament, that implies relationship. You cannot love one with whom you are not in relationship. Jesus tells us, therefore, that the most important thing we are to do in life is to love God, which is to say we are to be in a relationship with God based on love—not fear, not obligation or "duty," but love! In fact, Jesus tells us we are to call God "our Father." The word *Father* underscores the notion of being in a relationship with God.

Then Jesus says we are to love our neighbors as we love ourselves. The second commandment, which is like unto the first, is that we are to love those with whom we are in community as we love the One who birthed us into community! Once again, the notion of relationships is underscored biblically. We cannot love our neighbors if we do not love ourselves. Our relationship with our self is based on the *a priori* fact that we are made in the image of God. So we are made whole, and we are made human by the love of God and by the grace of God. Relationships are key. Relationships are foundational. Relationships are fundamental. Relationships are what make life truly life!

The African philosophical principle, which talks about the importance of relationships, says the same thing. From Liberia to Angola, the West African people embrace the principle that is captured best in the words of Dr. John Mbiti, who says that Africans who are Yoruba, Ga, Fanti, Akan, Ashanti, Fulani, Ibo, and Ibibio all teach, *"I am because we are, and because we are I am!"*

In West African thought and philosophy, personality formation is based on the principle of community, communal relationships, and living together with others. Whereas European epistemology is based upon the Cartesian principle of *cogito ergo sum* (which is, "I think, therefore I am"), the African understanding of personality formation does not have any notion of the first person, singular pronoun "I" but depends on the understanding of my personality being tied up with a "we."

Whereas European epistemology is based on a principle of autonomy, African epistemology is based on the understanding of community! Being in relationships is what makes being a human being.

The Zulu in South Africa teach the same principle. South African society is based on the principle of *ubuntu*. Its truths are captured in the saying *umntu, gumntu, gbantu*. That saying means an individual (*umntu*) can only be fully human (*gumntu*) by virtue of being in relationship with other individuals (*gbantu*).

The biblical principle is underscored in Zulu philosophy (which predates the Bible) by use of the word *ntu*, which is found in all three words of the sentence and in the key concept of community (*ubuntu*). *Ntu* means the breath of God, which is to say that an individual cannot be an individual without the breath of God.

An individual cannot be fully human without the breath of God, and no community can be what it was meant to be without God's breath infusing it, binding it together and making it what God meant for it to be when God created humankind. Without God's breath we are nothing more than flesh. Our *relationship* with God makes us human, and our *relationship* with others makes us what God created us to be.

Both the biblical teachings and the African teachings are saying the same thing: relationships are foundational. Relationships are key. We need relationships to be truly alive.

Dr. Kevin Cosby makes the biblical principles and the African principles come alive on the pages of this book. Dr. Cosby says the same thing that the Bible says and that African philosophy says in 21st Century African American language.

Dr. Cosby says that our relationships with each other and our relationship with God are the determining factors in terms of our destination, our aspirations, and our realizing our full potential. Cosby argues accurately that if a child is loved in infancy and in its toddler stages, that child will know love, experience love, and be able to express love as an adult.

He goes on to demonstrate that if the child is starved of love, however, that child will not be able to love others fully, nor love himself or herself wholesomely because the "community" that robbed that child of love will have marred and scarred that child for life.

Dr. Cosby isolates the problem of male absence in the African American family as one of the key problems that has to be addressed by and solved by the church community—the extended family! If a child is not loved by his/her daddy, and if a child does not realize who his/her daddy is, then that child wanders away from home, pulls away from the heavenly Father, and walks away from his/her own true personality. That child suffers what Orlando Patterson calls "natal alienation!"

Dr. Cosby demonstrates dramatically on these pages how a healthy realization as to who we are as God's children will create a healthy and wholesome personality that does not disrespect life, disrespect God, or disrespect others who are made in the image of God. Realizing that God is our "Daddy," Kevin Cosby argues, enables us to fulfill the potential that God has placed within us when God breathed into our nostrils the breath of life.

Dr. Cosby opens up the meanings of the parable of the Prodigal Son to demonstrate, irrefutably, that relationships are all important. Relationship determined the ultimate destination of the younger son—who wandered away from home but later realized the importance of that relationship with his father and returned home only to discover that his father had never stopped loving him.

Dr. Cosby argues that the foundational understanding of being in relationship with our father (*Who's Your Daddy?*) will enable us to live as God intended. He then shows how failure to develop a wholesome relationship with our "Daddy" will cause us to wander off, as the son in the story wandered off from his father. Failure to cultivate and appreciate that relationship with our "Daddy" makes us distance ourselves from God and from who it is that God made us to be.

Combining the skills of a trained homiletician with the experience of one whose life has been touched by the hand of God, Dr. Cosby helps us to see the importance of our relationship with God and our relationship with others.

Honing the hermeneutic of an African American male who is clear on his relationship with God and clear about his responsibility to live in community with others because of his relationship with God, Dr. Cosby takes the words of Jesus' parable on the Prodigal and makes them come alive in the 21st Century. Embracing the principles that Dr. Cosby articulates in this book will change your life forever!

Your relationship with God is key. Your relationship with God will determine the quality of your relationship with others and your ultimate destination in this life and the life to come.

Jeremiah A. Wright, D. Min.
Pastor Emeritus
Trinity United Church of Christ
Chicago, Illinois

The Story:
The Prodigal Son

Jesus went on to say, "There was once a man who had two sons. The younger one said to him, 'Father, give me my share of the property now.' So the man divided his property between his two sons. After a few days the younger son sold his part of the property and left home with the money. He went to a country far away, where he wasted his money in reckless living. He spent everything he had. Then a severe famine spread over that country, and he was left without a thing. So he went to work for one of the citizens of that country, who sent him out to his farm to take care of the pigs. He wished he could fill himself with the bean pods the pigs ate, but no one gave him anything to eat. At last he came to his senses and said, 'All my father's hired workers have more than they can eat, and here I am about to starve! I will get up and go to my father and say, "Father, I have sinned against God and against you. I am no longer fit to be called your son; treat me as one of your hired workers."' So he got up and started back to his father.

He was still a long way from home when his father saw him; his heart was filled with pity, and he ran, threw his arms around his son, and kissed him. 'Father,' the son said, 'I have sinned against God and against you. I am no longer fit to be called your son.' But the father called to his servants. 'Hurry!' he said. 'Bring the best robe and put it on him. Put a ring on his finger and shoes on his feet. Then go and get the prize calf and kill it, and let us celebrate with a feast! For this son of mine was dead, but now he is alive; he was lost, but now he has been found.' And so the feasting began.

In the meantime the older son was out in the field. On his way back, when he came close to the house, he heard the music and dancing. So he called one of the servants and asked him, 'What's going on?' 'Your brother has come back home,' the servant answered, 'and your father has killed the prize calf, because he got him back safe and sound.' The older brother was so angry that he would not go into the house; so his father came out and begged him to come in. But he spoke back to his father, 'Look, all these years I have worked for you like a slave, and I have never disobeyed your orders. What have you given me? Not even a goat for me to have a feast with my friends! But this son of yours wasted all your property on prostitutes, and when he comes back home, you kill the prize calf for him!' 'My son,' the father answered, 'you are always here with me, and everything I have is yours. But we had to celebrate and be happy, because your brother was dead, but now he is alive; he was lost, but now he has been found.'(Luke 15:11-32 GNT)

Introduction:
Addressing Prodigality

I could have no greater joy than to hear that my children walk in truth. (3 John 1:4)

The great state of Kentucky has and has had some excellent NCAA coaches. At the University of Kentucky there was basketball coach Tubby Smith. At the University of Louisville there is Rick Pitino and head football coach Bobby Petrino. If I were to have a roll call of some of the great coaches we've had in American sports, past and present, a plethora of names would surface, like Vince Lombardi, "Bear" Bryant, and John Thompson.

But where has the best coaching taken place? Not at a sports arena that holds tens of thousands of fans and not at a church youth league game. The greatest coaching takes place under your roof. "Why is that?" you may ask. If you're asking that question, then I need to ask, "Do you know who you are?" If you are a parent, get a whistle because you are coach-parent. That's what you are. A coach. That's all parenting is—coaching. The word *coach* originated in the 16th century; it was a word used to describe a horse-drawn buggy that took passengers from one place to another place. What is the main cabin of an airplane called? Coach. Why? Because when you get seated in coach, the airplane takes you from one point to another. So whether you are a coach-

1

mama, a coach-daddy, a coach-grandmother, a coach-grandfather, or a coach-uncle or aunt who's been appointed coach by heaven's Athletic Director, you cannot abdicate your responsibilities as head coach to someone else.

Part of my motivation for writing this book on lessons from the Prodigal Son is to help people gain the tools necessary to coach and to be coached through life. Anyone who knows the rulebook, the Bible, and follows it, will be well coached and will be well-equipped to coach others. It is my hope that having more good coach-parents will help to reverse the downward spiral of our young people and even many of our adults. With more good coach-parents, we will not continue to mass produce prodigals—bright young men and women who waste the advantages they have been given in search of frivolity. Prodigality is a part of everyone's spiritual maturation process; however, the key is to know how and when to return home to the Father.

The third epistle of John is all about coaching. John coached a disciple named Gaius. In chapter one, verse one, John wrote to Gaius, "My dear friend whom I love in the truth." Gaius became a Christian under John, his coach. Later Gaius became a pastor. After he had been coached into the faith and into the service of the Lord, John wrote to him. "Dear friend, you are doing a good work for God when you take care of the traveling teachers who are passing through, even though they are strangers to you." After having such an excellent coach, Gaius was challenged to begin coaching others. It's true for everyone that whatever you are and whatever you have become, it has been because somebody coached you. And since somebody coached you, when you see someone else in need, you're supposed to coach them.

To further grasp my point, consider 2 Timothy 2:2, which reads, "You have heard me teach many things that have been confirmed...." Paul was telling Timothy, "You've heard me teach, Timothy. Now teach these truths to trustworthy people." You've heard me teach; now you turn around and teach others, because once those trustworthy people have been taught, they will teach others. Thus, sound teaching perpetuates and builds a stronger faith community. That's how the church in the New Testament grew from 120 charter members into 100,000 members in 25 years—experiencing exponential growth. Once one person was taught, they lived according to this principle: each one reach one; each one teach one. This is an important philosophy of the faith because when God blesses you, He doesn't want you to close up and keep that blessing to yourself. He expects you to be a channel and a conduit of blessings for somebody else. So when you see somebody who's wearing white shoes in November, don't make fun of them; coach them. You'd be doing the same thing if somebody had not coached you. I do it all the time, especially with my children and their friends. For example, when somebody calls my house and asks for my son, saying, "Uh, is Kevin there?" I respond, "Yes." And then we just have a pause because they're not using proper telephone etiquette, which is, "May I speak with Kevin?" If they don't catch on, then I help them by saying, "Did you mean may I speak with Kevin?" But knowing these kinds of things comes from coaching.

It's the responsibility of parents to do that, but parents can't teach what they don't know. You have to be mature in the faith to know these things because you can't pass on what you don't have. I believe that the reason so many of our kids are falling behind educationally, socially, and economically has nothing to do with the people we love to blame—other folks like the police, the prosecutor, the judge, the teacher, the principal, or "The Man." The problem is that many parents are abdicating their responsibility to coach their children. They need coaching; it works, and I can prove it.

Have you ever noticed how tight-knit Jewish families are? Have you also noticed that you seldom read or hear much about Jews being arrested? Think about it. You don't hear about it, though it's not because society loves Jews. A study in recent years showed that in Florida, there were 40,000 people in jail. Only thirteen of them identified themselves as Jewish. Now, I'm not denying the reality of injustice or systemic oppression. But while we like to picket and protest, we need to be picketing parents because a lot of the challenges of our people have to do with culture.

Unfortunately, our culture is missing far too many fathers—making the title of this book *Who's Your Daddy?* even more relevant to our situation. In the mid-sixties Daniel Patrick Moynihan, who was then the Assistant Secretary of Labor under President Lyndon B. Johnson, issued a disturbing report on the state of the Black family. His "Moynihan Report" invoked an angry and hostile response from a host of the African American community's intellectuals. Essentially, the Moynihan Report determined that the Black community in general and the Black family in particular were in danger of peril due to the increasing number of female-headed households. Moynihan reported a trend that "more children are being born out-of-wedlock, often to girls that are still in their teens," and "if something is not done to arrest this problem, the future of the Black community is in great peril." Ironically, what caused the anger at Moynihan's report was neither his data nor his statistics, but instead it was the fact that he attributed the cause to something pathological within the Black family unit itself. He did not blame suspended racism and the impact it had on the family. So many sociologists attacked Moynihan's theory without examining the legitimate critique that he made of the emerging structure of the African-American family unit—namely, that too many of our families are matriarchal.

If I am anything, I am a realist. I know that we have to accommodate what we have based on the situation. Nevertheless, the ideal family unit is comprised of a mother and a father working together for the sake of the children and the family. Matriarchy is totally unacceptable, but one reason females have risen in their headship of African American families is due in part to the fact that the Black male in the 1960s found it more difficult than ever before to find jobs. Throughout the 1960s and 70s, many of the traditional jobs that our males used to occupy—International Harvester, the railroad, Ford, General Electric, and the Big Three automobile manufacturers in Detroit—were eliminated because of economic competition from other countries. Factories began shutting down, and many men lost their jobs. Most men have been socialized to believe that a man is not truly the head of his house if he is not the primary breadwinner. So scores of men opted to leave their homes and their women. Others became intimidated because the women were making more money than they. There are men who can recognize and accept that if his wife is making $40,000 and he is making $30,000, together they have $70,000. But many male egos are as fragile as eggshells.

In leaving their homes, young men had to learn what it means to be a man. We men opted to leave, entrusting family leadership to the hands of our females. Furthermore, because of the intricacies of entitlement laws, many of our families were penalized for having a man in the home. Having a man in the home would disqualify them from any type of federal assistance. So the man of the house would leave or be put out so that the woman and the children could receive benefits. When the man left, he paved the way for the social worker and the welfare agency to become Daddy. The children would look at the biological father and call him "Uncle Daddy."

Even though this has happened among our people and our families, we should never be satisfied with this type of family unit as the norm of our culture. In a family there needs to be a mother and a father. There will not be any community renewal until we revitalize and make functional our dysfunctional families. An important part of our ability to become functional depends on our ability to nurture our children into mature, productive members of society. Therefore, before moving into the life coaching tips to be learned from the Prodigal Son, I want to offer a few principles for coach-parenting.

PRINCIPLE ONE
Accept Your Child's Uniqueness

Every child is different. No child, not even an identical twin, is a carbon copy of another. Although Jacob and Esau were twins, they were different. Cain and Abel were brothers, but they were different. When you accept your child for who that child is, you build his or her confidence. Don't fall into the trap of trying to mold your child into your image or someone else's. Find out how they have been uniquely gifted and encourage the greatest use possible of those gifts. You wouldn't say, "I squeezed this apple but didn't get any orange juice to come out." You wouldn't get upset if you squeezed an orange and couldn't get grape juice out of it. So why expect your children to be anything other than who and what they are? This is not to say that you cannot challenge them to be better or try harder. Always encourage them to be their best and to push past their comfort zones. At the same time, it's futile to try and force them into being who they are not. If your daughter is good with her hands and wants to be a mechanic, it's foolish to try and force her to be a ballerina.

God has put something special in each of us, whether it is to be an electrician, a surgeon, a chef, a minister, or a computer technician. The goal and responsibility of the coach-parent is to nurture and mold what's on the inside until what is inside of them emerges.

Principle Two
Structure Your Child's Life

Every child needs structure. They need a specific time to eat dinner, to do homework, to go to bed, and to turn the television off. They need to know structure like an army regimen. Now, if you don't believe me, you can always tell how your child is doing by looking in his or her folder, for kids who do well usually have an organized folder, and their work is structured—English papers neatly put in the English section, math papers neatly put in math section and so forth. Conversely, a child who's failing will most likely be disorganized with a folder full of paper airplanes and doodles. Children who are structured most often come from households where there is structure.

PRINCIPLE THREE
Entrust Your Child with Responsibility

When you do things *for* people, you take responsibility *from* them. This is true of children also. They should be taught that privileges are earned. If they want money to go to the movies, make them earn it. So if your child's room is not clean and the garbage is not taken out, the movies should be a definite no-no. Make them earn it. This is especially true for mothers and their sons. There's a difference between mother and smother. Many mothers do everything for their sons, failing to recognize that one day they're going to be somebody's husband. By trying to be good mothers, many women mistakenly cripple their sons from growing up and becoming men. Instead they end up looking for "mother" in their adult relationships.

PRINCIPLE FOUR
Affirm Your Child's Value

There are many juvenile delinquents out there who were merely craving their parents' attention. How do you give your children your full attention? When they want to speak to you, give them your attention, eyeball to eyeball. Affection means hugging them and telling them you love them. How many women are walking the streets today because they never had a daddy to say, "I love you"?

PRINCIPLE FIVE
Correct Your Child Without Condemnation

Human beings are wired funny. We remember criticisms more than we remember compliments. For example, if six members of St. Stephen come up to me and say, "Pastor, I love your suit," but one person says, "That color doesn't look too good on you," I'm going to remember the one critical comment and not the six compliments. Children need correction and discipline; however, it's extremely important to balance your criticism of them with compliments. Even when they really mess up, correct without condemnation. Always leave them knowing that they still have value in your eyes and in the eyes of God.

Principle Six
Expect the Best

Have high expectations for your child. As a young man, I had an important experience that turned me around academically. When I was in the seventh grade, I was a marginal student. By the eleventh grade I had a history teacher who motivated me to learn. I started off making A's and B's in her class, but I slipped into making C's. One day she called me aside and said, "Kevin, if you get anything less than a B in my class again, I'm going to call your parents." When she told me that, I left her class feeling like I was the greatest person on earth because what she was saying to me was she knew I was better than a C student. Other teachers may have accepted C's from me, thinking, "Well, he's a Black kid, so that's probably the best he can do." But because she expected more, I delivered more.

Many times our kids don't do better academically because we don't expect anything better. You've got to raise their standards, which may begin by raising your own expectations of them. St. Stephen Baptist Church is located in the poorest neighborhood in Louisville. Yet people are amazed when they see our facilities—well-kept grounds, high-tech equipment, and a state-of-the-art family life center. We are sending a message even through our facilities that we expect the best for ourselves, and we give our best to the Lord.

Far too many people, young and old alike, don't expect God to bless them. They don't realize that they have greatness inside of them, yet because they don't expect anything, why should they expect God to do great things? Have some expectations of your children and teach them to have expectations of themselves. Teach them to get excited about what God is getting ready to do. We are to expect great things from God—expect deliverance, expect blessings, expect healing, expect peace, expect joy.

PRINCIPLE SEVEN
Never Give Up on Your Child

No matter what other people say, don't give up on your children because God is not going to give up on them or you. No matter how much you've messed up, God has never given up on you.

With these seven principles, you can grow to be a successful coach or coach-parent. People don't need Nike shoes, RocaWear, or FUBU to live and be happy. There is nothing wrong with having these things, but all you really need is God's Word and faith in Him. By doing this, you will discover *Who's Your Daddy?*

WHO'S
YOUR
DADDY?

Who's Your Daddy?

One day I was hand wrestling my twenty-one-year-old daughter. She put her fingers between my fingers, and I pushed down on her hand until she got down on her knees. While she was down on her knees, I looked at her and said, "Who's your daddy?" Sometimes life has to get us on our knees before we recognize who our daddy is. As long as we are under the illusion that we are capable of independence from our father, we tend to get brought down to our knees, and this is exactly what happened to a young man in Luke 15.

The parable of the Prodigal Son is one of the greatest stories ever told. Interestingly, the word prodigal never appears in the story. The word *prodigal* means "wasteful," and history has given that name to the son who went off to find fame and fortune, using his father's money. Yet the focus of the story told by Jesus is not the Prodigal Son, but the father. It is the father's incredible depth of love and forgiveness that lies at the heart of the story. Through this story, we learn that we can never get so far out there that God doesn't want us back.

When someone says the word *God*, that word conjures up different images in people's minds. If I were to say "God" around some people, they would respond by saying, "There is no God." Those are known as atheists. If I were to say "God" around certain camps, those camps would respond, "I'm not sure if He exists."

They are called agnostics because an agnostic is someone who doesn't know whether God exists. If I were to say "God" around some other people, they would say that He is someone to be feared. They are called fundamentalists because a fundamentalist believes in a vengeful God, a punishing, vindictive God. But if I were to say "God" in the presence of Jesus, He would say, "Oh, Father," or even "Daddy," because that is the consistent word that fell from the lips of Jesus when He referred to God.

The first recorded words of Jesus are these: at twelve years old, He said to His parents, "Did you not know I must be about my father's business?" The last recorded words of Jesus from the cross are "Father, into Thy hands I commend My spirit" (Luke 23:46). His first recorded words acknowledged His Father, and His last words acknowledged His Father—like two bookends with everything else in between. The Father and Jesus both invite us to relate to God as Father.

Who's Your Daddy?

What kind of father is the heavenly Father? Before answering the question, let me pause here and issue a theological disclaimer. God is so much more than we can ever know, so whatever I say about God, it is said with the recognition that God is so much greater than whatever can be said about Him. No one person can capture the "all-ness" of God any more than you can capture the Atlantic Ocean in a teacup. But there is one thing of which we can be certain: at the close of this examination of the Prodigal Son, God will be no less than what Jesus says about Him in the parable.

What makes the story of the Prodigal Son so significant is that it mirrors all of us in some fashion. The Prodigal Son is really about the lifecycle that we all find ourselves in. We are all in a lifecycle as it relates to God. This fellow, this rebellious young man, starts off at home in a solid relationship with his father. They engage in daily and regular communication. That's the way we are supposed to be—in a relationship with God. Christianity is about a relationship, not about religion, rules, or ritual. It's possible to be religious, but not have a relationship with Christ. For example, you can take the Lord's Supper, but that doesn't necessarily mean that we have a good and healthy relationship with the Lord.

FROM RELATIONSHIP TO REBELLION

The son in this story has a relationship with his father because he's at home with his dad. But then he has this itch to be on his own, to be independent of his father. Perhaps, he had imagined what it would be like to be the head of his own household, to make his own rules to obey, not his father's. So the son goes to his father and says, "Father, give me the portion of goods that is due me. Give me my inheritance right now. I want to leave and be away from you." He is rebellious against his father. He leaves home and rebels.

There is a time in all our lives when we have been rebellious—living in rebellion against God. Someone once said that sin and rebellion are simply Christians giving God the finger. For example, when God tells you to do something, like tithe or stop sinning and you don't, in a sense you're just giving Him the middle finger. That's all sin is. That's what this young man did in the parable. He broke his father's heart. We break God's heart when we rebel against Him. Rebellion always leads to ruin. When you rebel against God, you will ultimately experience ruin. This fellow is going to go down to a status that no good Jew would want to have—feeding hogs. He had gotten down so low that not only was he feeding the hogs, but he was so hungry that he wanted to eat what the hogs ate. So he was living lower than a hog.

When you rebel against God, you'll end up either in the hog pen or the state pen, but you're definitely going to the "pen." Rebellion against God always leads to ruin. In making this statement, I fully recognize that there are some people who have rebelled, but they have yet to experience ruin. Well, if you jump out the window of a downtown building, by the time you get to the fourth floor, you may be saying, "Wow, I'm down to the fourth floor, and I haven't had any problems so far." Right now, there are some people living on the fifth, fourth, third, and even second floor.

When the Prodigal Son had reached his lowest point, he decided, "I've got to repent. Boy, I've got to get out of this situation." So with that revelation, he went from ruin to repentance. Repentance is the only thing that can take us out of spiritual ruin. Repentance is saying, "Lord, I'm wrong and I'm sorry. I should not have done that. Give me another chance. Lord, have mercy on me." And He will, but anytime you repent, you always have to put feet to your prayers. So the Prodigal Son repented and got up out of the hog pen and said, "I'm going back home."

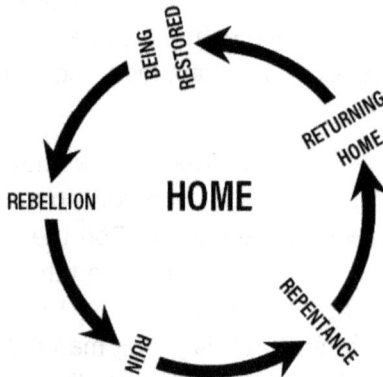

BEING RESTORED

RETURNING HOME

REBELLION   **HOME**

RUIN

REPENTANCE

The Prodigal Son had no idea how his father was going to receive him because he had messed up. But when he got home, his father overwhelmed him with love and compassion. And then the son experienced restoration. Now, any person can just about plot his or her life based on the lifecycle that the Prodigal Son experienced because everyone is at one of these life stages: either at home, in rebellion, in ruin, in repentance, returning home, or being restored. Every one of us can put a little mark on one of those lifecycle points and say, "This is where I am." It's important to know where you are because in order to get anywhere when you are lost, you first must find out where you are.

When my wife and I were in Orlando, we had to return the car we'd rented. We were lost, so I called the car rental company on the cell phone and told them, "We can't find you." Amazingly, the first thing the person said to me on the phone was, "Where are you now? I can get you where you need to go if you can just tell me where you are now." You've got to admit where you are. I said, "Well, right now we are next to this 7-11 or something like that." The rental agent said, "I know where you are now," and then gave me directions to the car return lot. But I never could have gotten to my destination if I had not admitted where I was while I was lost. "Where are you?" was the first question God ever asked. The first question God asked Adam was, "Adam, where are you?" And He is still asking all of creation, "Where are you?"

EGOTISTICAL PRAYER

Now notice this fellow is praying to his father. Any time you say something to your Father, it constitutes prayer. Luke 15:12 (KJV) is a prayer: "The younger of them said to his father, Father, give me the portion of goods that falleth to me." Notice that he is praying an egotistical prayer. Why is it an egotistical prayer? He made himself the center of the universe. It was a selfish, "me-centered" prayer. When you are me-centered, you are off-centered. When you are stuck on yourself, you will be stuck with you, and no one will want you but you. The Prodigal Son prays two prayers. On his way to ruin, he prays, "Give me." On his way toward restoration, he prays, "Lord, make me."

Psychologists assert that all of our emotional problems are rooted in an unhealthy, self-centered preoccupation with ourselves. If you get depressed, the true remedy is to find someone worse off than you and try to lift that person up, and you will get lifted up in the process. Whenever I have visited a sick person, when I pray for them, I always leave the hospital feeling better than when I first arrived. You get blessed when you take your mind off of yourself.

This self-centered son prayed a good churchy prayer. We love to be churchy—look churchy, talk churchy, act churchy. We love to say words like, "God, hallelujah! The anointing breaks the yoke!"

This is church jargon—church ghetto language. And do you know why he sounded so churchy? How do we know that it is a churchy prayer? Because churchy prayers always contain the name Father. The word *Father* can hide or camouflage a selfish prayer. In other words, stop being churchy with God.

When you relate to God, you should relate to Him as you would a friend. You don't talk to friends in a churchy way. For example, when my son wants something from me, he doesn't come to me and say, "Dear Father, husband of Barnetta, provider and sustainer of the family, wouldest thou in all thy benevolence grant me the keys to thy car that I mayest pick up my friends that we might go riding, dearest Sir?" He doesn't do that. He says, "Hey Dad! Hey, Man, are you going anywhere this weekend? I want to use the car." He just relates to me in a very natural way.

God wants His children to relate to Him in an unpretentious, natural way. I love to hear people talk to God in church like they are talking to a friend: "Hey God, I'm mad as hell but I love You." Just keep it real. I was considering putting a real message on our church marquee: "Accept Jesus. Hell sucks." When I told my son what I was thinking about doing, he said, "Dad, that's hip. That's hip."

The son in Jesus' parable reiterated his self-centered prayer to his father. That means there's more emphasis on me than there is on the father. Do you pray egotistical prayers? A servant's prayer is, "God, use me. What do you want me to do, Lord?" Those are the kind of prayers God wants to hear from His people, not those selfish prayers. "Seek ye first the kingdom of heaven...."

ENTITLEMENT PRAYER

An entitlement prayer is a prayer in which you ask God to do something for you, without your acting with God to bring it to pass. An entitlement mentality says, "You owe me. I'm entitled to certain things, and I don't have to work for it." The Prodigal Son didn't say, "Daddy, give me a job," or "Daddy, give me an opportunity to earn some money." He didn't ask his father for an opportunity to work for what he wanted. You should never ask God to give you something that you are not working to answer. For example, if you ask God to get you out of debt but you keep spending or keep running up your credit cards, then you are praying an entitlement prayer. If you ask God to heal your marriage but you won't go to counseling or make any concessions, you are making an entitlement prayer.

There is nothing worse than an entitlement mentality, thinking that people owe you something without your having to do your part. Without God I cannot, but without me He will not. The quicker you realize that nobody owes you anything in life, the better off you will be. There was a family taking a family portrait when the photographer said, "Young man, why don't you put your arm around your dad to make the picture look more natural?" The father said, "Yeah, well why don't you tell him to put his hand in my pocket; that will really make it look more natural!"

Your children are supposed to have their hands in your pocket because they are children and are your dependents. But as they start getting older, it's time for them to take their hands out of other folks' pockets.

Ironically, sometimes parents want children to keep their hands in their pockets because if they can keep their children's hands in their pockets, that is their way of manipulating and controlling their children. Some parents still use money and things to control their children at thirty, thirty-five, and forty years old. You are only a successful parent when your children grow to be capable of standing on their own two feet. It is your responsibility as a parent to work yourself out of a job.

EMPTY PRAYER

This fellow wanted his daddy's money because he wanted to leave home and have some fun and happiness. He had the bright lights of Las Vegas twinkling in his eyes. He wanted a lot of money so he could go to Vegas, because he'd heard that is where all the happiness is. There is nothing wrong with wanting to be happy. God planted in you the desire to be happy, but the problem comes when you go to the wrong places looking for the right thing. Happiness is not found in Vegas.

There was one occasion of a Christmas party where people were exchanging gifts. A guy was calling names and saying, "Come and get your gifts." Now, there was a big box with wonderful wrappings, a beautiful bow, and glitter. The man it was meant for grabbed the box totally excited and said, "Thank you!" He opened the box, pulled back the wrapping and inside was nothing. Somebody had played a cruel joke on him. Somebody had put his name on a box with ribbon and glitter on it to make it look pretty. But when he opened it up, there was nothing inside. In this world, you must be careful because the world is filled with empty boxes. We work hard, sacrifice much and compromise our integrity just to get that pretty, empty box. What is in the box that you want? A job? A relationship? So often in life we get a pretty box, and we get all excited. But once we open it up, we find out that it's empty.

The Prodigal Son wanted to leave home because he saw a beautiful box with bows and glitter. He thought, "If I could just get that shiny box, if I could just leave home and do my own thing in Vegas, I could be happy." He wanted the right thing but was going to the wrong places to get it. His father gave him the money. But when he got to Vegas, all he experienced was ruin and emptiness. This fellow went all around the world looking for what he already possessed. If you have God, you've got happiness because happiness comes from being in a relationship with Him.

Freddy the Fish washed up on shore. Some of his friends walked by and asked, "How are you doing, Freddy the Fish?" Freddy answered, "Oh, I am so frustrated, so depressed." His friends asked why. He said, "I don't know. It's just that something is missing, and I don't know what. I don't know what's wrong with me. I can't figure out what's missing. But you know what? I saw a commercial on television about a brand new German-made car. If I could just get one of those German-made cars, I would be happy." So they took Freddy to the dealership, and he bought the German-made car he wanted. His friends saw Freddy the Fish the next day, and he was still unhappy. "What's wrong?" they asked. He said, "I don't know. I can't figure out what is missing. I'm so frustrated and depressed all the time. I don't know what's wrong. But I saw a commercial on television that talked about a credit card that would give me unlimited spending power. If I could just get that credit card with unlimited spending power, I know I would be happy." Freddy got the card, but the day after he got it, he was still unhappy and frustrated. He had a German-made car and an unlimited credit card, but he was still frustrated. Freddy kept on searching for and acquiring things that he thought would end his unhappiness and frustration—liquor, sunglasses, a tattoo on his fin, a gold grill in his mouth, and gold chains around his neck. They gave him a year's subscription to *Playfish* magazine with those beautiful, fine catfish in the middle of them. But his friends were still asking, "What's wrong with Freddy the Fish?" What did Freddy need? He needed to get back home in the water. You will never be happy until you get back home to God.

There was a fellow from Tennessee who told one of the greatest preachers on the planet today, Fred Craddock, this story:

Let me tell you a good preaching story. I grew up not far from here in East Tennessee. When I was a boy, I never knew who my daddy was. My mother was a teenage mother, and not only did I not know who my daddy was, my mother did not know who my daddy was. I was the scandal of the community because in those days to be without a father was a disgrace in this small Bible Belt town.

He went on to explain:

Everywhere I went, I saw people pointing at me saying, "He doesn't know who his daddy is." I wanted to go to school, and the kids who had both parents would say, "He doesn't know his daddy is." I lived under a cloud of shame. So one day I went to church, and there was a new preacher in the pulpit, a tall preacher with a deep, baritone voice. It was my habit to sit in the back and dart out when the benediction was announced. But on this particular Sunday, the preacher gave the benediction early. When he did so, there was a crowd in front of the door, and I didn't have a chance to get out. So there I was, trapped, trying to get through the crowd.

Suddenly, someone tapped me on the shoulder. I was twelve years old at the time. It was the big preacher! I looked up at him, and he looked down at me with his deep voice and said, "Young man, how are you doing?" I said, "Fine, Sir." He said, "Well, whose son are you?" I could have gone through the floor. In school, "Who's your daddy?" On the street, "Who's your daddy?" Around the family, "Who's the daddy?" And now I had come to God's house, and the man of God was asking me, "Who's your daddy?" But that preacher sensed that I did not know who my daddy was because I hesitated. He looked down at me and said, "Ah, I know who your Daddy is. You look just like Him. Your Daddy is God. That's who your Daddy is. And since your Daddy is God, you have quite an inheritance. Go, Boy, and claim your inheritance."

And the man said, "That preacher telling me who my Daddy was changed my life." The man who told the story was Ben Harper, three-time governor of the state of Tennessee, whose life was changed simply because he knew who his Daddy was.

Who's your Daddy? God is, of course. Go claim your inheritance because He can hardly wait to see you!

How Far Is
The Far Country?

Years before anyone had uttered a word about conservation, reclamation, or the foolishness of littering when I was about eight years old, I learned an unforgettable lesson about the proper disposal of paper products. My parents stopped at a corner grocery store in our neighborhood in the West End of Louisville. When my mother went into the store, I decided to go with her. I stood next to the section where the candy was, just staring at a Payday candy bar. I turned to my mother and passionately and aggressively begged Mom to buy me that Payday. Normally, my mother was the type of woman who would never, ever succumb to such a trivial request. But to my joyful amazement, on this particular night my mother caved in. She bought me the Payday, and I returned to the car, gleefully clutching my candy bar in my hand. When I got in the back seat, we drove off, and I ripped the wrapper off the candy bar. In my excitement, I threw the wrapper on the floor of the car, which left me with a Payday candy bar that was attached to a cardboard casing. Well, I took the cardboard casing off the candy bar, and instead of throwing it on the floor or placing it in my pocket, I made a dreadful mistake. I had the cardboard in one hand and the candy bar in the other, and I don't know what happened, but I got mixed up, and instead of throwing the cardboard out, I threw my prized candy bar right out the

21

window. As soon as I let it go, I immediately realized the horrific mistake I had made—especially as I looked out the back window and saw the candy bar fade into the darkness of the night.

That was almost forty years ago, but the experience made such an impression on me that if you were to ask me today, "Kevin, what did you get for your birthday when you were eight years old?" I couldn't tell you. Or "Kevin, what did you get for Christmas?" I couldn't tell you that either. But four decades later, I can still remember in vivid Technicolor the awful anguish, the emptiness, and the sleepless night I had when I realized that I had thrown away the very thing I had wanted so badly. I was left with nothing but a cardboard casing.

I remember that episode in my life whenever I see a Payday candy bar. I remember it any time I see someone throwing something out of a car window. I remember that episode whenever I read this story about the Prodigal Son. Here's a fellow that had something far more valuable than a candy bar in his hand: he had possession of a good life in his hand, and he threw it away. When he came to himself, the only thing he had was a spot in a dirty, degrading hog pen. At that point, he decided to go home and throw himself on his father's mercy.

But he needed to go through the experience. The son had gone to his dad and said, "Dad, give me the money that befalls me. Give me my inheritance." He had grown tired of sowing corn in the country. He wanted to sow some wild oats in the city. There are still folks who want to sow wild oats in the city. A lot of folks sow wild oats all during the week and then come to church and pray for a crop failure. His father gave him the money, and the son left the country. He had money in his pocket, but no sense in his head. As soon as he saw the flickering neon lights of the city, he said to himself, "Let the good times roll!" He lived in the fast lane—sleeping by day, partying by night. He wasted his father's money on what Jesus described as riotous living. He had lots of friends while he was ballin', but then the money ran out. When he had money, he had plenty of friends, but once his funds were low, his friends became few. He had squandered all of the money, yet he could find no one to give him any aid. So he took a job doing something no respectable Jew would ever do—feeding swine in a place the Bible calls "the far country."

"Where is the far country?" you may ask. "Is it very far away?" Well, it's not as far away as you might think. In fact, you may be closer to the far country than you realize, especially if you consider that the far country is more of a condition of the heart than a place on the map. The far country is more spiritual than it is spatial. It's more about disposition than it is destination. But just like a roadmap, there are certain attitudes that lead us to the far country, and if you possess certain attitudes, you might be living right next to far country county. What are the attitudes that lead a person to the far country?

INGRATITUDE

Let me give you a very specific and clear definition of what ingratitude is. Ingratitude is when you are blessed and fail to recognize that you're blessed. That's ingratitude. Ingratitude is when you've got it going on, but you don't appreciate what you have, and you let it slip through your fingers. Ingratitude will take you to the far country faster than anything else. You see, this fellow had it going on, but he didn't appreciate it. He had a remarkable, loving father. He had a great heritage and had great hope, but he threw it away because of ingratitude. Whenever you are ungrateful, you are close to the far country. Therefore, it's important not to let ingratitude seep its way into your heart. How does ingratitude get a foothold? You can get ingratitude in your heart because of two realities.

First, we live in an imperfect world. The farm that the son lived on was not a perfect farm. He had a daddy that was a good daddy but not perfect. He had a brother who was a nag and a drag, so it wasn't a perfect environment. Granted, imperfection mars everything. There are disadvantages in every climate because of imperfection. There are thorns on every rose. There are faults in every friend, every husband, every wife, every parent, every child, every job, every employee, and every employer. Everywhere you go, anything you do, and everything you see has imperfection. There is nothing perfect about anything we touch. So the home where this boy was with his daddy was a good place, but it wasn't perfect. And that's true about every human experience.

Second, we have been endowed with a critical faculty. God gave you the ability to be critical and analytical, or discriminating. God has given us the ability to say, "No, that's not good and, yes, that is good." That is called a critical faculty. It is a God-given gift in order to see imperfections and correct them, to see wrongs and right them. If you weren't able to be critical, you wouldn't know the difference between a watermelon and a seed. But because you can make critical assessments, you can say, "No, I don't want this seed, but I do want this watermelon part."

Our critical faculty is helpful in our human existence; therefore, it is a good thing to be critical. You grow from criticism. You grow as a woman or man because someone has been critical of you. You grow as a person because of honest self-criticism. That's all repentance is. Repentance can be understood as taking a sightseeing tour through the departments of your interior—seeing that things are not the way they should be according to God's standards and saying, "I need to make some adjustments." You would never make any adjustments if you didn't possess the capacity to be critical.

Woe be unto anyone who loses the right to be critical. Woe unto the husband whose wife can't say anything to him. Woe unto any wife whose husband can't say anything to her. Woe unto any child who doesn't receive honest, constructive criticism at home. All of us grow as a result of criticism. God gives criticism for correction, but we must be careful with our criticisms. When misused and abused, criticism turns destructive instead of constructive. It becomes lopsided, and we can easily overshoot our goal. We can focus on the negative and what is missing and lose sight of the good. It's almost a natural human impulse to say what we don't have, but we need to be careful. It's an impulse that, if taken too far, can make us blind to what we do have, and then we lose a good thing.

In life there's always something you can complain about. If you spend ninety-five percent of your time complaining about problems, you're going to be a problem. But if you start counting your blessings, you're going to be a blessing. If you have an ache, instead of focusing on the ache, thank God that at least you can get up and feel something. If you have problems on the job, instead of focusing on the problems or the things you don't have, thank God that at least you have a job and a steady paycheck. Thank Him for what you have, while focusing on new opportunities to move to another job. Instead of complaining about your spouse, you should focus on the positive qualities of your mate and your marriage.

There's a story about a dog that was carrying a good-sized hambone in his mouth. As he was going to bury his bone, he spied another dog carrying a hambone. He looked at the other dog's bone, which looked a lot bigger. He decided to go after the other dog's bone. As he prepared to attack the other dog, he fell into a pond and lost his prized hambone in the water. After he fell in, the dog realized that he had been looking at his own reflection all along. For some reason, the bone had looked bigger when he thought that it belonged to another dog.

You can look at the five percent that is wrong in your life, and only focus on that five percent, and be blinded to the ninety-five percent that's right and functioning well. It happens in people's lives. People think their lives aren't worth living because they're focused on the little that's wrong instead of on the lot that's right. It happens in marriages, also. Let me use a female perspective to illustrate my point. Let's say that a woman has a husband who is generally a good man, but he's not very romantic. In fact, he's so romantically challenged that on one occasion she snuggled up to him and asked, "Baby, do you love me?" He replied, "I told you I loved you twenty years ago when we got married, and if anything changes, I'll let you know!" He never brings flowers home. He never comments about how good she looks. One day she put on a new dress, and she wanted him to marvel over her. She asked, "Hey, Baby, does this dress make me look fat?" He responded,

"Naw, Baby, it's your hips that do that." He has no romantic impulse or instinct, but he's a good man.

What should his wife do? In many cases, the wife will focus on the fact that her husband is not romantic and tell her girlfriends how sick and tired she is of her unromantic mate. This dialogue may sound familiar: "I feel like I'm in a prison. My husband never says anything good to me about me, and I am a woman. I am sick and tired of other men telling me that I look good, and my husband never says anything about how I look good."

Meanwhile, the girlfriend is encouraging her, "Oh no, Girlfriend! Honey, I wouldn't put up with that stuff. You need to get rid of him!" Then the wife goes to work and meets up with a smooth talker. She loves to run into him because she knows that she is going to get her ego stroked. He always tells her how good she looks. He tells her that her hair looks good. He asks her how she is doing. He tells her that she is looking good and wonders if she has lost some weight. All of that attention makes her giddy and wanting more. She starts thinking, "I like that. I need to be appreciated. I deserve someone who makes me feel good about myself." Before she knows it, he starts talking really nice to her on a regular basis. She says to herself, "If only my husband would do that, then I'd be happy." So now she crosses some boundaries and breaks her marriage vows only to realize that her smooth talker has five percent romance and is ninety-five percent con.

She finds herself in the far country because her husband is over here in the land of commitment and fidelity in marriage, and she is in a different place. Then she wonders, "How did I get here?" Only after she loses her husband does she realize that, while he wasn't romantic, he came home on time, their kids were stable, she didn't have to worry about the utility bill, and they were working together. Instead of her complaining about the five percent, she should have been celebrating the ninety-five percent. Meanwhile, the friend who was telling her not to put up with that stuff has now gone after that hardworking husband she's lost.

Whenever you are so critical that all you do is talk about the five percent you're lacking, you're going to lose your Payday. You are throwing your Payday out the window. That's true for both women and men who just complain about their spouses and never say anything complimentary. That's also true about children, friends, careers, and anyone or anything that we care about.

No matter how bad or how lacking you think your life is, you can still count your blessings. It's easy to count your blessings when you realize that you have houses that you didn't build, vineyards that you didn't plant, and wells that you did not dig (see Deuteronomy 6:11). Not only that, but when you praise God, you start feeling better. That's why Paul and Silas were praising God in their prison cell. Even in jail, Paul declared that he had made a choice to rejoice in the Lord despite his circumstances. The devil can't stand praise because he wants you to feel sorry for yourself. The devil always wants you to feel down.

IMPATIENCE

Another thing that will get you into far country is impatience. Luke 15:12-13 reads: "The younger of them said to his father, Father, give me the portion of goods that falleth to me. And he divided unto them his living. And not many days after the younger son gathered all together, and took his journey into a far country" (KJV). The father gave his son real property. He took the property and converted it into cash—then took the cash and went to a far country where he spent it on riotous living. When did he go to the far country with the cash? Six months later? No, verse 13 says "not many days after."

His father had given him his inheritance in the form of real estate. But since he could not take the real estate to the far country, he had to convert it into cash. He only waited a day or two before selling. So what does that mean? Normally, it takes more than a day or two to sell property. But if you are in a hurry to sell real estate or if you are in a hurry to get a car without searching around for the best deals, you come out on the losing end. And that always leads to the far country. Impatience can send you on a quick trip to the far country.

When you catch this disease called "hurry-up-itis," you jump into things because you're desperate. You want to get into things without saying, "Wait a minute; I'd better check this thing out before I jump into something." The quick fix doesn't always fix. Many people are in the far country right now—emotionally, psychologically, and financially—because they jumped into something when they should have waited. We jump into some things prematurely. We live in a culture that accelerates everything. You think that you must have what you want when you want it. No one can wait on anything. Even when you go into the kitchen, everything is microwavable or precooked. We have electronic mail, fax machines, overnight mail, text messaging, picture mail, mobile phones, and Slim Fast. If you need money, you can go to the ATM, or go get some instant credit. "Get it while you wait... No money down... and 90 days same as cash" are all familiar slogans to encourage a quick buy from an impatient mind that craves instant gratification.

In the field of agricultural technology, they have fertilizers to speed up crop production because no one wants to wait. They feed protein to hens to get them to hurry and lay that egg. They give them hormones to get bigger faster. In baseball they used to lift weights, but now it just takes too long to lift weights and get muscles the way Willie Mays, Hank Aaron, and Joe DiMaggio did. So they take muscle-enhancing drugs called steroids to "get buffed" quickly.

People are impatient to build wealth so they stand in line at the gas station or convenience store to buy lottery tickets—causing delay for the few people who actually want gas. Youth are impatient for the chance to live like adults. Today, young people want at nineteen what it takes a working man or woman fifteen or twenty years to build.

Everybody's looking for a shortcut to paradise. But things that are valuable, that last, and that really mean something don't come overnight. You've got to be willing to wait for some things. Any time you are in a hurry, you are on your way to the far country. So what will get you to the far country? The answer: ingratitude, impatience and, finally, inconsideration.

INCONSIDERATION

The Bible says (verse 13): "And not many days after, the young son gathered all together and took a journey into a far country and there wasted his sustenance." Now, it was his daddy's money; the son didn't work for it. He took what somebody else worked for and wasted it. Daddy had plowed in the fields, planted, and gathered for that money, but his son was a waster. That's what the word prodigal means—waste. In the story, there are two men: a father who is a worker and a son who is a waster. We have that in society today. Some people are workers; other people waste what others have worked for. Nothing should anger you more as a parent than when you have worked hard to get your children some things, and they waste what you have worked for. Father is a worker, and the son is a waster.

I had an occasion to listen to a hip-hop awards show at which Minister Louis Farrakhan was given an award. Minister Farrakhan said to the hip-hop artists and all the scantily-clothed women sitting on the stage: "This generation: you the greatest hip-hop artists that our people have ever produced—are the greatest generation to emerge from the African-American experience because you have created a music, a genre that has connected people globally. People are listening to hip-hop globally. You are the greatest generation our people have ever produced." I love Minister Farrakhan, but when he said that, I felt a revolt in my system. You mean to tell me that Ludacris and 50 Cent are the greatest we have produced? I think not!

I believe that the greatest generation we ever produced was the generation of Dr. King because they were workers. The reason you can vote is because they were the workers. The reason you can be employed in corporate America is because they were workers. The reason you can go to any school you want is because that generation was a class of workers that desegregated colleges and universities across the nation. The reason Condoleezza Rice and Colin Powell rose to leadership in the White House is because their generation was the workers.

Commenting about this proclivity to idolize and iconize the slain artists, Biggie Smalls and Tupac Shakur, Chris Rock said,

Wait a minute. You cried over Tupac and Biggie Smalls. You wear T-shirts with their picture on it. You want to make them a cultural icon and role model. I know that they are dead, but let the record be clear: they were not assassinated. Martin Luther King and Malcolm X were assassinated. Viola LaRuso, the white Detroit woman who came down South to help in the Civil Rights Movement, was assassinated. Medgar Evers in Mississippi was assassinated. Goodman, Schwerner and Chaney were assassinated. Tupac and Biggie Smalls were not assassinated. Those Negroes just got shot!

He said there is a difference between getting assassinated and getting shot. Workers get assassinated.

So if Dr. King's generation was the workers, guess what this generation is? The wasters—because we are wasting what they worked for. They worked for the right to vote, and you waste it by not going to vote. They worked to get you in school, and you wasted the opportunity by acting like a clown in class. Martin Luther King, Jr. did not go to jail for us to be wasters. Rosa Parks didn't sit down for wasters. Mary McLeod Bethune didn't go digging through garbage to get chairs for wasters. Goodman, Schwerner, and Chaney didn't do what they did for wasters. Fannie Lou Hamer didn't protest for wasters. This generation is wasting what sit-ins accomplished and freedom riders got humiliated for.

What defines a *waster*? A waster can rap but can't read. A waster can make a baby but can't make a bed. A waster can curse on the corner but can't answer a question in the classroom. If all someone can do after Martin Luther King, Jr. took a bullet for his people is "drop it like it's hot," that person is a waster. Every time an African American sits at home on Election Day, that person is a waster.

Luke 15:14 also says that after the Prodigal Son had spent all of his father's money, "There arose a mighty famine in that land;

and he began to be in want." Waste and want go together, because any time you waste, you always produce want. If you have the opportunity to get an education and you waste it, ten years later, you'll be wanting it because waste goes with want like macaroni goes with cheese. Famine came and his money ran out. He had nothing in his pocket and no skills. He should have taken the money and enrolled in college or gone to a vocational school to learn how to do some plumbing. But this brother chose to waste the money, trying to be a gangster, "pimping his ride."

When hard times came, with no job and no skills, he had to take a job feeding hogs. He was really scraping the bottom. Remember, this story was told to a Jewish audience, and Jews don't eat pork. In fact, pork was an unlawful and prohibited sustenance in Jewish society. A Jew could go to the penitentiary for having pork. So the only work he could find was engaging in illegal trafficking of substances called hog meat. He became a part of the pork mafia. He was on the corner, and his beeper was always going off, because while no one was supposed to be smoking ham, there was an underground market for a dime bag of smoked ham. He would stand on the corner, and folks would page him. People would ask him if he had a gram of pig feet or a kilo of pork crackling. They had what they called bacon blunts. So he ended up in the hog pen, and he got there because of his ingratitude, impatience, and inconsideration of what someone else had worked for, which he wasted.

The official slogan of the United Negro College Fund is, "A mind is a terrible thing to waste." Our forebears understood the value of an education. A blessing is also a terrible thing to waste. Some of us have tremendous blessings that we take for granted— being raised by loving, albeit imperfect parents; living in a nice house, although not the largest in the neighborhood; having a good job, even though the job is not without some problems. These are the blessings that we overlook.

A poet once wrote:

Once I had mountains in my hands
and brooks that flowed along the way.
I must have been mad.
Didn't realize what I had until I threw it away.
I must have been mad.
Didn't know what I had until I threw it away.

Here's the good news. If impatience will take you to the hog pen, then patience will keep you. If ingratitude will take you to the hog pen, then saying "Thank You" is good spiritually and psychologically. Praising God will keep you out of the hog pen. Count your blessings. Live a thankful life and stop complaining all the time. Balance your life and find something to be grateful for.

How to Get Out of Swineland

Sometimes it's a good idea for Christians to visit a homeless shelter just to become sensitized to how low a person's life sometimes can sink. It may seem ironic, but as much as we see stories about the devastation of humanity on television, some people are still living in a state of ignorance about the way of the world. While most people realize that there are problems and unsavory elements in the world, for the most part, even in the midst of our troubles, most churchgoers live on "Nice Street." We interact with nice people. But not everyone lives on "Nice Street." Anyone who doesn't believe it will soon find out that truth after just one visit to a shelter. Going to a homeless shelter will not only remind you of how low humans can sink, but also of how vast the love of God is. Going to the shelter can give you insight into just how far down God's power can reach to redeem and rescue someone who has fallen just as deeply as the Prodigal Son had fallen when he came to himself in the pigpen. Think about that: God's power is able to reach down into the hog pen to redeem and rescue those who are lost.

One homeless man who got saved at a shelter recalled, "The minute that I got saved, I lost 70 percent of my vocabulary!" We sometimes forget that many of the great heroes and heroines of our faith were not "stained-glass" saints. They were not the saints

33

that we have replicated in the stained-glass windows of our cathedrals. Rather, most of the great heroes of our faith—Paul, Peter, Matthew and others—were once hog pen dwellers that God delivered. Saul of Tarsus wasn't always the apostle Paul. Before he met Christ on the Damascus Road, Paul was the "Osama Bin Laden" of the first century. The first systematic theologian that the church ever produced was an African from Hippo whose name was Augustine. And although he was the first to systemize the doctrines and tenants of the Christian faith, Augustine did not always live according to the doctrines he wrote. Augustine was so steeped in vice and debauchery that no one wanted to associate with him except his mother! But God reached down and touched Augustine while he was in the cellar of humanity.

Moving closer to contemporary times, there was a man by the name of John Newton, a man who rejected his heritage and his culture and went off seeking adventure on the seas as a vagabond and as a slave trader. He trafficked human cargo. While out on a slave ship one day, in the middle of a terrible storm, God reached down and touched John Newton in his hog pen, and Newton was authentically converted. Following his conversion, Newton dipped his pen in the inkwell and poetically wrote these words:

In eve alone I took delight,
Unerred by shame and fear,
Until a new object struck my sight,
And stopped my wild career.

You may be unacquainted with the poetry of John Newton, but practically every member of Christendom recognizes the second verse of the poem:

Amazing grace, how sweet the sound,
That saved a wretch like me;
I once was lost but now I'm found,
Was blind but now I see.

These transforming works, perhaps the greatest Christian anthem in the history of the church, were written by a slave trader who had spent a great deal of his life in the hog pen. Within the lives of Paul, Augustine, and Newton lies a timeless truth, amplified in the story of a young man who broke his father's heart and squandered his father's money on riotous living. The message in the story of the Prodigal Son teaches us this: No matter how far you have dug yourself down into the pit, you can come back. And no matter how far out you have gone—and human beings can get way out there sometimes—you can still come in. No matter how far down you have sunk, you can come up.

In the story of the Prodigal Son, we find a young man who has gone down as low as a person can get. He's so low that he has to have a ladder just to reach bottom. He started off with a whole lot of money in his pocket and no sense in his head, living high on the hog. But he quickly went from living high on the hog to living underneath the hogs. In telling the parable, Jesus identifies three things that the young man lost while he was out there in *Swineland*. Luke 15:14 (KJV) reads, "And when he had spent all, there arose a mighty famine in that land."

Lost Fortune, Food, and Friends

The Prodigal Son lost his fortune because he wasted all his money. He was broke. Verse 16 reveals: "He would fain desperately have filled his belly with the husks that the swine did eat" (KJV). When he lost his fortune, he not only lost his money; he lost his ability to get food to eat. He was hungry, and in those days they were not allocating EBT cards. He could not get anything to eat. But what about all of those people who were hanging out with him while he was living large and partying his daddy's money away? The last portion of verse 16 reads, "and no man gave unto him," which means he lost his friends. So the Prodigal Son lost his fortune, he lost his food, and he lost his friends. He had friends when he had money, but they were fair-weather friends at best.

It's easy to attract friends when you have money. But the hallmark of a true friend, someone said, is somebody who is in your corner when you are in a corner. A friend is somebody who walks in when everybody else walks out. The only friends the Prodigal Son had after he lost his money were some pigs—some unclean friends. Have you ever had an unclean friend? One of our deacons at St. Stephen is known for not eating pork. Occasionally, we go out to eat together or we have a repast after church, with ham sandwiches or green beans with a healthy dose of jowl bacon. Usually, I'll fill my plate and then look at him and ask, "Man, you want some of this ham sandwich?" And his classic response is, "That swine ain't no friend of mine!" I'm sure the Prodigal Son would agree with that deacon: "This swine ain't no friend of mine! They're too dirty to be friends."

The Prodigal Son wanted the food that the hogs ate, but the hogs were so dirty and greedy they wouldn't even give him the scraps. Every time he went over to the trough to get a husk, one of the swine would "pimp slap" him. Ain't that something? Pimp slapped by a pig! That's pretty bad, isn't it?

This boy's experience should drive home for all of us the devastating consequences of sin. The devil would have us to believe otherwise, but sin always has consequences. Even when you are forgiven, the consequences of your sin are not erased. The Prodigal Son would eventually get up and go back home, but some things he would never get back. He would never recover his father's money. Perhaps, he had a girlfriend before he left his daddy's house and went to the far country. And while she liked him a whole lot, after he went way out there, she had to go on with her life. She met somebody else. And though he prayed in the name of Jesus, "Forgive me," his prayers couldn't undo the fact that the girlfriend he left had gone on with her life. It could just be that he contracted some venereal disease during his many escapades in the far country. And though God forgave him, it would not eliminate the disease—because sin has consequences. There are three things that sin will always do, which the Prodigal Son learned while in the far country:

1. Sin will always take you farther than you want to go.

2. Sin will always keep you longer than you want to stay.

3. Sin will always cost you more than you want to pay.

Allow me to illustrate: Let's assume there was a time in your life when you were sowing wild oats. (A whole lot of believers sow wild oats and then expect the preacher to pray for crop failure!) But let's assume that you were sowing wild oats, and you wanted what you wanted, in the words of the late balladeer Luther Vandross, "only for one night." All you were looking for was just one night, huh? Six weeks later you get a phone call: "Hey, I'm pregnant." You only wanted one night, but sin took you farther than you wanted to go, and now you're about to be a daddy. Instead of the one night you wanted, you have to be associated with that one night fling for at least another eighteen years. You never intended to be associated with her for eighteen years; it was only supposed to be for one night. She never intended to be associated with you for eighteen years either; but now you're stuck with each other for another two decades or more because your sin will keep you together. To complicate matters even more, one payday you look at your check and think, "Wait a minute, they done cheated me out of my money!" That's when you realize that your sin that was supposed to last for only one night is now costing you more than you wanted to pay—child support. Sin will cost you.

GOD'S LADDER OF REDEMPTION

Despite the negative scenario I've reviewed, there is good news: regardless of the hog pen you may find yourself in, God is always willing to stretch a ladder down far enough to help you climb out. This ladder that God stretches down into your hog pen has five rungs on it, and you have to be willing emotionally and physically to climb up on each one of the rungs. If you're trying to climb out, just remember that God wouldn't put a rung where He didn't give you the grace and the power to climb up. He's going to give you a ladder with five rungs on them.

1. REGRET

The lowest rung of the ladder is very basic—regret. The first rung of the ladder is the emotions you feel when the weight and the gravity of what you have become hit you. Rung one is when you start thinking about what you had and where you allowed your decision-making to lead you. You start saying things like:

> *"If only I had not hooked up with her."*
> *"If only I had not hooked up with him."*
> *"If only he/she had not ever come into my life."*
> *"If only I had hung up when God told me to hang up."*

"If only, if only, if only ...," that's regret, the first rung. If you are feeling some regret about sin and your poor decisions, that's a good starting point—but only a starting point. Many believers climb on that first rung of regret, and they stay there for ten years. All they do is stay in a state of regret, lamenting a past that cannot change or be undone. When you squeeze toothpaste out of a tube, there's no use crying about your inability to get the paste back into the tube. There are some things that once done, can't be undone. Therefore, spending ten years regretting what you cannot undo is a waste of emotion and energy. It's stewing without doing. It's like starting your car and then pressing on the accelerator but never putting the car in drive. You've used a lot of gas and made a lot of noise, but you haven't gone anywhere.

The real problem with wasting your emotions is that you won't have them available to you when it's time to deal with the real issues of your life. For example, if someone doesn't like you, don't trip. Wasting your emotions on people you cannot change is not worth the time and energy it takes to do so. Instead, go on to bed and get some sleep. Give that person or situation over to the Lord instead of wasting your energy and thoughts on things that you cannot change.

2. REMEMBER

It's good to grasp the first rung of the ladder, but at some point, you have to move on past regret. If you're going to climb higher, you have to go the second rung of the ladder—remember. Verse 17 (KJV) reads: "And when he came to himself, he said, How many hired servants of my father's have bread enough and to spare, and I perish with hunger!" The Prodigal Son never forgot who he was. He never forgot that although he was with the hogs, he wasn't one of them; he was the son of a great man. Even though he was in the hog pen, he knew that he was not a hog because of who his daddy was. Back in the sixties, there was a television program called *Bonanza*. It was about a rancher named Ben Cartwright. He had bank-fat pockets. Ben Cartwright had a nice ranch home. Ben Cartwright had land and cattle. Ben Cartwright had power and respect in the community. He also had three sons, and because they were Cartwrights, they walked with dignity. They knew that their daddy's name was Ben Cartwright. Even Hoss, the son who didn't have a whole lot of brainpower, walked with dignity because of who his daddy was.

Remembering who your Father is helps you, especially when you're stuck in the hog pen. But sometimes while you're there, people will try to convince you that you really are a hog and that you should be content living a hog's reality. They might say something like, "What's wrong, boy? Why are you complaining about the mud? This is good mud; it's cool mud. It's got just enough insects and crunchy bugs in it to give you all the nutrients you need." The hogs might say, "What's wrong with these bugs? These bugs taste good. What's wrong with this slop, boy? You think you're too good to eat slop or something?" The Prodigal Son couldn't identify with the hogs because he had a higher pedigree. The reason why you will never be comfortable living like a hog is because of who you are. You've got a higher pedigree. There are some places you are not supposed to be just because of who you are.

At some point, the Prodigal Son began to remember his true identity. He must have told himself something like, "My father is Ben Cartwright, and I'm getting up out of here! My father's servants live better than this." Now to whom was he talking? He was talking to himself. The most important conversation you will ever have is the conversation you have with yourself. Ultimately, it's not important what people say to you, but it is important what you say to you. People may say, "You are no good," but that's just their opinion. It's only a problem if you say that you are no good. There are some people who will say, "She'll never make it," but that's just their opinion. As long as you don't say it to yourself, you can make it. That is why the most important conversations you have are the conversations you have with yourself.

Sometimes I talk to myself while I'm walking in the mall or down the street. I love to talk to intelligent people, so I talk to myself! I love to hear intelligent people talk, so I listen to myself! I talk to myself like the Prodigal Son was talking to himself. He had two parts of his personality—the lower self and the higher self. Each of us has a higher self. I have a higher Kevin, and I have a lower Kevin. The lower Kevin is always talking with the higher Kevin, debating on what we are going to do and in which direction we are going.

It reminds me of my sister, Janice. When I was younger, any time my sister was kind, I said, "Thank you, J Nice." But whenever she was mean, I would say, "Forget you, Jan Ice!" Like her name, her personality had two extremes in it—nice and ice. Now, while every name cannot be parceled and broken into syllables like that, our personalities can be parceled in a similar way. Your character can be broken down into two components. You've got some *ice* in you, and you've got some *nice* in you, and whomever you allow to dominate the conversation in your head is who wins out. So when somebody mistreats you, *Nice* says "Forgive them. Pray for them." Meanwhile, *Ice* is saying, "Cuss them out! Clock 'em! Give them a piece of your mind."

Well, the *Nice* in the Prodigal Son started talking to *Ice* and said, "Look, Ice, the reason we're in the hog pen in the first place is because you have dominated the conversation. So you shut up,

Ice, because Nice is running the show from now on." Nice decided, "Wait a minute, we have to go back to Daddy!" That's the second rung on the ladder—remember.

3. REPENT

After you remember, it's time to move on up to the third rung on the ladder—repent. In verses 18-19, the Prodigal says, "I will arise and go to my father, and will say unto him, Father, I have sinned" (KJV). Of all the rungs on the ladder, this third rung is the hardest. Of all of the rungs you must climb, this rung is the most difficult, but also the most critical—because in this rung you are assessing blame for how you got in the situation you are in. In America we live in a "no fault" society—no-fault insurance, no- fault divorce, etc. Nobody wants to take responsibility. In fact, we have the agility to dodge personal responsibility for the pit in which we find ourselves. We say, "The reason I'm in a pit is because somebody pushed me in. I wouldn't be in this pit if So-and-so didn't do such-and-such to me." The truth is that nobody can put you in a pit against your will. There are folks who may have contributed to your pit, but they weren't the cause of your pit. You need to give up those lame excuses like, "She makes me sick," or, "He's going to make me clock him."

Nobody has the power to *make* you do anything. They may tempt you to do something, but if you do it, you will do so only because you choose to do it. Most people love to blame other people for their predicaments. A husband who was in counseling with his wife said, "Oh yes, I'll be happy to split the blame for our failed marriage. It's half my wife's fault, and the other half is her mother's fault." Rarely do we hear someone utter, "It's all my fault." But in order to get out of the pit, you've got to confess your wrongdoing, "God, it's not my mama; it's not my father; it's not my sister; it's not my brother; but it's me, it's me, it's me, oh Lord, standing in the need of prayer. It's me, I'm wrong. Nobody made me do it. Nobody made me take that drink. Nobody made me step outside the boundaries of my marriage. Nobody made me steal. Nobody did it to me."

As hard as that kind of gut-level confession may be, it's also liberating. If you blame other folks, that means that you can't get up, that your life can't turn around, until other people change—something over which you have no control. And that's good news. Thankfully, your getting up out of the pit is not predicated on what someone else does. Your getting up is predicated on what you choose to let God do for you. No one else has to change in order for you to change. You can get up out of your situation because it is you who put you there. You put yourself in your own trick bag.

4. RETURN

The fourth rung of the ladder out of your pit is return. In other words, after you have regretted, after you have remembered, and after you have said, "Lord, I've messed up," getting to the fourth rung means you have to go back to your Daddy. Verse 20 tells us that the Prodigal Son arose and came to his father. There's something very important to note about the Prodigal Son getting up from the hog pen and going to his father. When he got up from the hog pen, he smelled like a hog. He was dirty, and he stank.

Today, most of us are far too domesticated, far removed from the farm to understand just how filthy a hog is. There's no animal that's as filthy as a hog. The Prodigal Son had been sleeping and eating with filthy hogs, which means he smelled like a hog when he got up. He had hog slop on him. He had hog residue all on him. His clothes were dirty; his hair was matted; his teeth had not been brushed; lice nested in his hair, and dirt oozed from his fingernails. If he still had on shoes, they were dirty, too. But as filthy, infested, and smelly as he was, he still got up and said, "I'm going to return to my father."

Notice what he did not say. He did not say, "I'm going to return to my father after I clean myself up." No, no, no, no! God doesn't want you to try and clean yourself up. God doesn't want you to say, "Well, as soon as I get myself together, that's when I'm coming back to church." God doesn't want you to try to get yourself together before coming to Him. God wants you to come to Him just the way you are. He will receive you, but He won't leave you the way you are. He wants you to come to Him just the way you are—no matter how filthy and smelly. He wants you to bring your drunk, high, gay, lesbian, coked up, cracked out self to Him just the way you are. You don't have to be all polished and sophisticated. You don't have to get your Sunday-go-to-meeting clothes on. You don't have to go get your hair coiffed. Come as you are, and if the people sitting near you act like they can't stand the smell of you, tell them, "I've got an invitation to come just as I am."

Sometimes we good church folk forget this, but the church is the only place where the prerequisite for becoming a member is: you have to be bad and in bad shape. For instance, if you want to join a fraternity, you have to sell yourself. If you want to become a part of corporate America, you have to sell yourself. If you want to join a local civic club, you have to sell yourself. But if you want to join the church, you must be willing to admit that you're no good. You've got to be dirty to join the church. A lot of people say things like, "There ain't nothing but hypocrites in the church." My response always is, "Well, where in the hell are they supposed to be?" There's only one place—the church. Nobody—not the choir members, not the deacons, not the ushers, not the trustees, not the associate ministers, not the pastor—has it all together, so we need to quit sitting in church looking all sophisticated and uppity. Like the Prodigal Son, all of us have come to the Father just as we are.

5. RECEIVED

The fifth rung of the ladder comes after you regret, after you remember, after you repent, and after you return: you are received. When the Prodigal Son returned to his father, he was received. Verse 20 reveals, "But when he was yet a great way off, his father saw him..." (KJV). What did the father do? The Bible doesn't say that he saw him a great way off and shut the door. It doesn't say that when he was a great way off, his father saw him and called the police, saying, "I've got a trespassing pig pusher on my property." The father didn't shake his head saying, "You disgusting son, I knew you'd come back wallowing in the dirt. You are pathetic!"

As the Prodigal Son made his return, it wasn't the preacher or the deacons who saw him, because preachers and deacons aren't always looking for lost folk. But even while the Prodigal was a great way off, his father saw him and had compassion on his smelly, dirty, wayward son. Upon seeing his son, something deep in the father was moved, and he received his son. That word "compassion" is *splagchnizomai*, from which we get the word "spleen" or "abdomen" or "inner parts." Have you ever felt something in your gut? When the father saw his son, something turned in his gut—because he had always been looking for his boy to return. Every morning when the father woke up, he would peep into his son's room and say, "Maybe he came back last night," but his son wasn't there. Yet he never gave up on his son. He never turned his son's room into a home office. He never took his son's plate off of the table. Every morning it was his routine to go out on the front porch and look down a long winding road in hopes that his son would be walking back home. After all of that waiting and hoping, one morning he went out on the porch, and in the distance he saw a figure coming down the road. At first he didn't recognize him because his face was covered with mud, his hair was matted, and his clothes were dirty and torn. At first, the father didn't recognize his son because the outline of his son's frame showed someone who was bent over. At first he didn't recognize his son because he walked with a limp. But the father then looked at him carefully and said, "That's dirt on him." But the more he looked, something dawned on him, "Wait a minute! That ain't a homeless boy. That ain't a pig pusher. That's my son!"

When he saw his son, the father jumped from the porch and did something that is seldom associated with God. This is the only time in the Bible where it implies that God runs—because God is never in a hurry. You never read about God running because God never has to run. God is eternal—yesterday, today and tomorrow. It's all happening right now for God. To Him, one day is a thousand years. But this time, God runs. I believe that God ran this time because any time someone wants to get himself together, God will get in a hurry and run to him. Not only did the father run to his son, the Bible says that he kissed his son. He kissed him with a crazy kiss. The son hadn't had a bath. He had lice in his hair. He was covered in pig filth, but his father was kissing him.

Every time somebody gets saved, God is kissing something dirty. Who's your Daddy? The question begs asking because some of us have some messed-up images of who the Daddy really is. Some people think of Him like the police officer who monitored my son when he took his driver's test. When he was sixteen years old, my son went to take the driver's test. He was already nervous and anxious because he knew there was a tradition in the Cosby family—no Cosby has ever failed the driving test. His mother had passed, his daddy had passed, and his older sister had passed. He was the last one to take the driver's test. While he was waiting his turn, I watched him and could tell that he was nervous. Suddenly, a big state trooper showed up and said "Your turn." My son was nervous because the state trooper had a clipboard in his hand, and he told my son "Get in the car." My son complied. Then the officer said, "Start the car," and my son started the car. The trooper continued giving my son directives in preparation for his driver's test. And he said, "Turn on the lights," and my son turned on the lights, and the man checked "lights" on the clipboard. I watched my nervous son as he complied with the officer's instructions, watching everything all the while. All during that time, the policeman never offered to give my son any help. He never offered to give him any advice. He just kept his clipboard in his hands, watching everything my son did, giving him a grade while saying "Check." The experience made my son feel uncomfortable, but it was a temporary encounter. Unfortunately, many people have an image of a daddy like that—a clipboard in his hand grading everything you say and do. Did you curse? Check. Did you lust? Check. Did you lie? Check.

Who's your Daddy? That ain't my Daddy! Let me tell you about my Daddy. My Daddy is a different kind of driving instructor. When I was a little boy about five or six years old, I looked at my father, and I asked, "Daddy, can I drive the car? Although he knew I couldn't drive his Chrysler, Daddy looked over at me and said, "I'm going to let you drive." He picked me up out of my seat, sat me in his lap, put my hands on the top of the steering wheel but kept his hands on the bottom of the steering wheel. Because my feet and my legs couldn't reach the brakes or the accelerator, my daddy helped me. He reached and did for me what I couldn't do for myself. When he said, "Turn, Kevin," I would turn. At the time I didn't realize that the only reason why it was a smooth turn was because my daddy had his hands on the bottom of the steering wheel.

Who's your Daddy? That's my Daddy! He put me in His lap. God put me in His lap, put my hands on the top of the steering wheel, kept His hands on the bottom of the steering wheel—and He's been steering for over sixty years. He's been steering. He's been guarding. He's been leading my life. Do you know who your Daddy is? If you know who your Daddy is, you can ignore the people who try to tell you that you can't make it. If somebody says you can't make it, look at that person and say, "That's your opinion, but you ain't my Daddy!" Some people may try to tell you that you're no good. Tell them, "You're a liar. You ain't my Daddy!" If somebody says you're down and can't get up, you can tell them, "You're a liar, and you ain't my Daddy!" Don't listen to somebody who's not your Daddy.

Your Daddy says, "Greater is He that is in you than he that's in the world." We know that all things work together for good for those that love the Lord. Your Daddy says, "Yes, weeping may endure for a night, but joy will come in the morning." That's shouting news for anyone who's ever been in a hog pen. Knowing who your Daddy is means understanding that you can never get so low that His grace cannot lift you up.

Don't Be a Dissin' Brother!

One day, many tax collectors and outcasts came to listen to Jesus, but the Pharisees and teachers of the Law started grumbling, "This man welcomes outcasts and even eats with them!" In response, Jesus told them the parable about the Prodigal Son. But while ol' Prodigal was off doing his thing, getting buck wild and partying like it's 1999, his older brother Frugal remained at home, working in the fields. When the Prodigal Son came home, Frugal was in the field working and hadn't gotten the news. On his way back to the house, he heard the music and dancing. He called one the servants to him and asked what was going on. The servant said, "Your brother is back, and your father has killed the prime calf because he came back safe and sound."

The older brother was so enraged that he wouldn't even go into the house! The father came and begged Frugal to come in, but he spoke back to his father, "Look, in all these years, I worked for you like a slave, and I have never disobeyed your orders. What have you given me? Not even a goat for me to have a feast with my friends. But this son of yours wasted all your property on prostitutes, and when he comes back home, you kill the prime calf for him!" The father explained, "My son, you are always here with me, and everything I have is yours; but we had to celebrate and be happy because your brother was dead, but now he is alive. He was lost, but now he has been found!"

How would you receive someone fresh from the hog pen? They'd still have the stench and the filth of the hog pen on them. Would you receive them into your circle? Would they be invited to sit on your pew? Would you welcome them into your ministry or auxiliary? Would you have room for them in your heart? Now, we don't have to ask how God receives people fresh from the hog pen because in this wonderful story of the Prodigal Son, we know that God receives with grace people straight from the hog pen or even the state pen.

When the Prodigal Son left home with a lot of money in his pocket and no sense in his head, he broke his father's heart. That was strike one. Strike two came when he squandered all of the money and had nothing left and no place to go. Finally, this homeless, penniless Jew ended up producing an illegal substance—hog meat. That was strike three. But then he came to himself and returned home. After returning home, the Prodigal Son realized that his father did not have a "Strike three" policy. When he came to himself and returned home, his father was ready to greet his son. The father saw him coming and rejoiced. He didn't call the police to have him arrested. He didn't go into the house and slam the door. He didn't berate him for being a failure and a squanderer. Even though the son was smelly, dirty, and had spent all of his father's money, the father leaped from the porch and ran down the winding road where his boy was walking toward the house.

With the stench and residue of the hog pen still clinging to him, his father embraced him and kissed him. Have you ever kissed someone who hasn't had a chance to clean up or brush their teeth? Not an inviting scenario, is it? Isn't it good that God kisses dirty folks? The boy had rehearsed a speech, but during all the kissing he couldn't even get the words out of his mouth before the father started snapping his fingers. The father commanded the servant to quickly get a robe and a ring for his returning son. He gave the son a signet ring. The father also instructed them to get him some shoes and to kill the fattest calf. "Let's be merry because my son I thought was dead is alive!" That is how God receives people straight from the hog pen, state pen, or any other pen.

But the question is not how God receives people from the hog pen but how we receive people straight from the hog pen. Certainly, we are not as magnanimous as the Father. In fact, the reason why Jesus told this parable was in response to the criticism that He had received because of the kind of folks He hung out with. Jesus was the champion of the *nobodies*. The religious folks, who were the *somebodies*, thought religion was always for the *somebodies* and never for the *nobodies*. In fact, they thought that in order to be in the church, sing in the choir, serve on the deacon board, be a missionary, or serve on an auxiliary, you had to have clean fingernails and fresh breath. They thought you had to have it all together, but Jesus had a counter-cultural movement.

Whenever Jesus would show up, He was accompanied by what the great mystic Howard Thurman called "the disinherited." Whenever and wherever He showed up, He offended the sensibilities of the religious establishment for allowing society's riffraff to associate with Him. For example, Matthew 10 describes some of his associates. Phillip, Bartholomew, Thomas and Matthew—the tax collector—showed up with Him (verse 3). Tax collectors don't win awards for popularity or good citizenship; they don't today, and they didn't in Jesus' day either. No one was hated more than tax collectors because they were collaborationists and thieves. Tax collectors levied taxes from their fellow Jewish citizens, so they helped to finance the occupational forces of the Roman Empire that was oppressing the Jewish people. They also overcharged the people, pocketing the excess for themselves.

So while Rome was oppressing the Jewish people, Jesus had a collaborator like Matthew in His *posse*. On the other end of the political spectrum, there was a zealot, patriot, and traditionalist (verse 4) named Simon, who was trying to overthrow Rome through force. Jesus was hanging out with an "Uncle Tom" named Matthew and a revolutionary like Stokely Carmichael, who was trying to overthrow the government. Jesus had Clarence Thomas on the deacon board and Stokely Carmichael on the trustee board. So that means Jesus showed up in church and offended everyone's sensibilities because He had Clarence on one end and Stokely on the other.

People will say, "We hate these guys." If that is not enough, each time Jesus showed up in church not only did He have Stokely and Thomas on His pew, but He also had a disgraced girl—Mary Magdalene. The Bible says that Mary Magdalene had seven demons. Seven is the number of completion, so that means if she had seven demons, she was completely messed up. So Jesus—the Lamb of God and God incarnate—showed up with Clarence Thomas, Stokely Carmichael and Lil' Kim. And if that's not enough, He had another guy hanging out named Zaccheus—Tupac. He also had another fellow named Peter who had tattoos all over the place and gold across his grill. Peter was a roughneck, Kentucky coal miner, Pittsburgh steel worker. His vocabulary was so profane that Lil' Jon and the Eastside Boyz would blush! The religious leaders saw Jesus with this riffraff and began to criticize Him: "One day when many tax collectors and other outcasts came to listen to Jesus, the Pharisees and the teachers of the Law started grumbling that this man welcomes outcasts and even eats with them" (see Luke 5:29-31). Jesus told them this parable of the Prodigal Son to respond to the criticism He had received because of whom He allowed to sing in the choir.

Usually when we hear the story of the Prodigal Son, we get the movie theatre version: the son returns home, the father runs off the porch, and embraces him, and they live happily ever after. At this point, the theme music plays, the lights come on, and the credits start rolling. That's when we get up to leave the theatre and say, "That was a good movie...touching." But Jesus says, "Wait a minute! Stay in your seat. The plot of this movie is really just getting started. The plot is not only to say something about the missing brother but also about the dissin' brother. I am telling the story to introduce church folk to themselves." What bothers Jesus is not the badness of bad folk but the unrecognized badness of good folks—good people who are just as messed up as the bad people but don't know it. That's why Jesus told this story.

The Bible says after the party had been going on for several hours, the older brother came in from the field and began making his way back to the house when he heard the music and laughter. This man had been working in the field, was tired and hungry, and needed a bath. When he came in from the field, he saw the light and heard the music. The sounds of R. Kelly's "Step" were playing and the line dancing took up the whole front yard. This brother smelled the aroma of the barbeque and saw the discarded watermelon rinds, chicken bones all over the place, and the stain of potato salad and green beans left on paper plates. He saw another trash bag filled with empty soda cans. He started thinking, "What in the world is going on here? Someone really important must be visiting for my father to put on a party like this." When he inquired about the occasion for the party, the servant told him that his brother had come home from the pen. The brother began to think, "All of this is for my brother? My brother!" He became so angry that his lip stuck out long enough for him to trip over it. He became the *dissin'* brother. One brother, the Prodigal Son, was the missing brother. But the older brother who had faithfully stayed close to home and worked in his father's fields became the *dissin'* brother.

DISSATISFACTION

Why call him the dissin' brother? Because he "disses" and disrespects everything—the people, the situation, and even his own circumstances. The first "diss" he is guilty of is *dissatisfaction*. Verse 28 states that the older brother was so angry that he would not even go into the house when he heard that the party was for his younger brother. God planted the emotion of anger in us, but how many people consider the fact that there is only one letter difference between anger and danger? Why is he so angry? Because his brother has been blessed! Now wouldn't you agree that is a mean spirit to have? His anger over his brother's blessing reveals his character flaws. But these character flaws have been camouflaged by social respectability. He's messed up on the inside, but no one can really tell because he has all the trappings of social respectability. He looks respectable. He goes to church, serves on committees, is a college graduate, respectfully cares for his father and his affairs, never causes any problems, is a member of the chamber of commerce, the Rotary Club, 100 Black Men, Black Achiever of the Year—and the list goes on. Underneath that veneer of social respectability is a heart salivating with envy.

This means there are always two kinds of sinners. There is the sin of action. The younger brother was struggling out in the world, and his own actions put him there. He was separated from the comfort of his father's protection and care because of his actions. There is also the sin of attitude. The dissin' brother was separated from his father, not because of any wrong action, but because he had a wrong attitude. Usually when we want to evangelize, we focus on witnessing to people who have the sin of action: those who drink, smoke dope, engage in promiscuous sex, are spousal abusers, etc. But we need to be equally vigilant in witnessing to those people who sin through their jacked-up attitudes. Those are the sinners who have never solicited a prostitute, never been drunk, and never been to jail, but they have a jacked-up attitude.

DISRESPECT

The dissin' brother has attitude—envy, self-centeredness, and social callousness. He was like the woman who said that she is allergic to fur coats. "Every time I see my girlfriend in her fur coat, I get sick." But the reason she gets sick is because of her attitude. The younger brother was the missing brother, but the older brother's attitude made him the dissin' brother. He was the dissin' brother, not just because of his negative attitude. Despite the fact that his father came out of the house and begged him to come inside, the dissin' brother then dissed his father! Why did he disrespect his father? He was mad at his father for being a prodigal-hugging father. The God we good Christians love so much is a prodigal-hugging God. We don't always like that. In the Bible, there are people just like this brother that do not like the fact that God hugs dirty, smelly prodigals.

The Old Testament prophet Jonah found out the hard way that God hugs prodigals. God told him to go and preach to the people of Nineveh, archenemy to the Hebrews. Jonah said he wasn't going to do it because he was prejudiced against Ninevites. So he got mad at God and went as far from God as he could in the opposite direction. Syria was in the east, and Spain was in the west, so he headed west by boat to get away from God. There was a storm on the water, and Jonah was thrown overboard. In the water, he had an ambulatory experience with a whale. The whale picked up Jonah and swallowed him in its belly. Stuck there for three days, Jonah finally relented: "God, I'll preach to those Assyrians." And the whale regurgitated Jonah and set him free. He grudgingly went to Assyria, yet when he reached the land of the prodigal people he didn't like, he preached a short message with no passion. He simply said that in seven days Nineveh would be destroyed. Despite Jonah's lack of enthusiasm, the Ninevites got saved anyway. And because they got saved, each one of them would go to heaven. When Jonah heard that God would embrace the people that he didn't like, he got upset. In Jonah 4, the prophet was angry with God for hugging prodigals.

The entire New Testament revolves around this one issue. The early church was essentially a Jewish church. They were not practicing "gracism;" they were practicing racism. In Acts 10, the Holy Spirit fell in excess upon an Italian, and he got saved. Jesus told Peter to go and preach to the Italian. But Peter said, "No Lord, I am not going to preach to them because I don't want to hug that kind of unclean folk." God told Peter, "You go preach to them, or you're fired as my preacher because I am a prodigal-hugging God." In life, there will be some folks that you just don't like, but that doesn't mean that God doesn't like them. Just because you don't want to speak to them doesn't mean that God doesn't want to speak to them. Why?—because God is a prodigal-hugging God.

DISREGARD

Like the heavenly Father, the father in the parable of the Prodigal Son is a prodigal-hugger. The dissin' brother confronted his father with what must have been a matter of resentment that he had been harboring for quite some time. "All these years I worked for you like a slave and never disrespected you. And what have you given me in return? You haven't even given a goat for me to have a feast with my homies." The son puts his ingratitude in plain view. He disregarded everything the father had done for him. At the beginning of the story, when the father gave the Prodigal Son his portion, Luke 15:12 indicates that he gave both sons their portions. The father divided unto *them* his living. The younger son asked, but both sons got paid that day.

In telling the story (see Luke 15:11-12), Jesus explained, "There was once a man that had two sons. The younger one said to him, 'Father, give me my share of the inheritance.'" The younger son requested it, meaning that the older brother would inherit something too. Despite this, the older son still confronted his father with a laundry list of complaints about how he had been deprived. He completely disregarded all of the blessings he had received through his father. He was connected to a successful father. He also had been given prestige, honor, a roof over his head, clothes on his back, a heritage he could be proud of, servants at his beckon call, and part of a successful business. But he was still complaining to his daddy. That's why envy is a dangerous thing. Envy will cause you to resent the blessings in someone else's life while ignoring the blessings in your own life.

The dissin' brother had disregarded all that his father had done for him. If you are blessed and you disregard those blessings, it's like not being blessed at all. For example, if you stuffed a $50 bill in your jeans last July and forgot, you still have $50. But if you don't know it's there, you are disregarding it. So you could be dead broke as far as you know—struggling, begging and pleading for just a few dollars to make it to the next payday—not realizing that you have $50 stuffed in a pair of jeans in the closet. If God has been good to you and you don't know it, that's like not having His blessings at all. The older son disregarded everything the father had done for him—all because of a party and a goat.

Not only did he disregard what his father had done, but he also disregarded how messed up he was in his heart. How can we know that he was messed up? In verse 30, he complained, "This other son of yours wasted his money on prostitutes." Wait a minute! He had been in the fields all day and hadn't talked to his brother. In fact, he hadn't seen him in a year. So how did he know the Prodigal Son had been with prostitutes? The passage doesn't tell us that. In the parable, Jesus said the son was with hogs, not whores. But the reason this accusation rolled off the dissin' brother's lips so freely is because he was guilty of what psychologists call projection, for in his imagination that is what he would have wanted to do. He simply projected onto his brother the actions that were really in his mind and heart. He disregarded how messed up he was.

This story reminds me of the work of blockbuster-movie producer Steven Spielberg. Every time folks watch a Spielberg movie, they miss the point. Spielberg, who is a Jew, realizes there are ethical principles in the Gospel, but he can't tell secular people about Jesus, so he has to back door them. *Saving Private Ryan* was a movie about a soldier named Jim Miller who dies while saving Private Ryan. Because Miller is wounded, Private Ryan lives. He is wounded for his transgression so he lives. We all have heard a story about somebody dying so that someone else can live. The movie *E.T.* was about someone from another world who befriends neglected children. Now, the authorities are threatened by E.T. so they persecute and murder E.T. The children are heartbroken because E.T. is dead. A few days later, however, E.T. comes back to life. After he comes back to life and proves to the kids that he is alive, he then says that he has to go home. In the last scene in the movie, E.T. is ascending a mountain. They are looking up at the clouds as he ascends. Have you heard that story?

In one of the most touching parts of the movie *The Color Purple,* Shug Avery, the wayward preacher's daughter, who has been out in the world, comes back home to the church. They bust the church doors open, singing, "God Is Trying to Tell You Something." Shug stands at the altar looking at her pastor/father, ready to embrace him and be reunited. But to whom has God been trying to tell something? It wasn't the daughter, the juke-joint Jezebel, but her father who had been serving dutifully in the church. While the daughter admittedly had bad behavior, the father in the pulpit with the robe on and the Bible in his hand had a bad attitude. God had been trying to tell him, "The reason that your daughter is out there is because you won't love and forgive her." God was trying to tell the *preacher* something because she busted into the church, singing, "God is trying to tell *you* something." When it hit the father, he had a light-bulb moment. He takes off his glasses because he is finally seeing the light. He walks down from the pulpit and comes down to her level. Ironically, her outstretched arms embrace him first, and slowly he puts his arms around her. Yes, God was trying to tell Shug something, and she got the point. What we miss is that God was also trying to tell her saved, sanctified daddy something.

DISAPPOINTMENT

The dissin' brother had a sin of attitude, dissin' everything and everybody because of his dissatisfaction, disrespect, and disregard. He was also a *disser* because of his disappointment. In verse 29, his father begged him to come inside and join the celebration. He responded to his father's invitation with, "Look, all these years I worked for you like a slave." Now, if you think that the Prodigal Son had broken his father's heart by leaving home and squandering all of his money, that paled in comparison to his older son's dissin'. He did not complain that he had worked all those years like a son, which is interesting because the motivation behind the work of a slave and the motivation behind the work of a son are different. A son does work for his father out of love and commitment.

A popularized scene from the movie *Fiddler on the Roof* comes when one of the peasant farmer's three daughters told him that she wanted to get married to the man she loved. But the father did not understand what love had to do with marriage. He did what he did for his wife and she did what she did for him because they were slaves to each other. He then went into the house and started singing to his wife, "Do you love me?" She sings back that all those years she had washed his clothes and cleaned the kitchen—yet he had to ask whether she loved him. But the husband sang again, "Do you love me?" The wife responded in song about all of those years that she milked his cows, farmed his land, and darned his socks. The husband sang his question a third time, and it finally dawned on her what he is saying: "With all that you have done for me, are you doing it out of love? You may be doing it simply out of obligation."

I believe that Jesus is asking every believer, "Do you love me?" We say, "Yes, Jesus. I come to choir rehearsal right after work even though I'm tired." But that's not what He is asking. Jesus is asking, "*Why* do you do it? Do you do it because you want to hang out with your friends? Or do you go to your church because it's the in-thing to do, and you can say that you're a member of a popular or prestigious church?" He wants to know: "If you sing, preach, or pick up paper in the church, why do you do it?" There's only one reason why you should do it: because you love Him.

DISTANCE

The dissin' brother had issues of dissatisfaction, disrespect, disregard, disappointment, and finally, distance. The father pleaded with his son to come inside the house, which meant that he was at a distance from the house. Not only can your actions separate you from God, but also can your attitude. The younger son was distanced from his father's house because of his actions; the older brother was distanced because of his attitudes. The father was eager for the older son to come inside the house so that he could enjoy both his sons and be a family again. The father answered his dissin' son, saying, "You are always here with me, and everything I have is yours. But we had to celebrate and be happy because I thought your brother was dead, but he is alive. He was lost, but now he has been found."

The Bible does not tell us whether the dissin' son came inside the house. Jesus left this parable as an open-ended story because the elder brother in the story is us—the church folks. This means you write the conclusion based on whether or not you are going to forgive someone you don't like. If people have hurt you or you don't like certain people, and God says, "Let's forgive them," and then you respond, "Oh no, God," that means you're distanced from God. But if you say, "God, they hurt me really bad, but I am going to forgive them," then you are in the house. God wants all believers to write the conclusion with someone from whom they are estranged.

What the dissin' brother needed more than anything was to come in the house. Inside the house was catfish, fried chicken, ice-cold Pepsi, watermelon, sparkling grape juice, and barbeque beans—with Marvin Gaye playing in the background. What he needed and wanted was inside the house, and the only thing that was keeping him from getting what he needed was his own attitude. His father was offering him what he needed, but he had to go inside the house to get it.

The same thing that was hindering the dissin' brother hinders us, too—attitude. I remember making a conscious decision not to let what people say about me or do to me cause me to spend one minute in bitterness. Worrying about what other people think has a negative effect on a person's attitude. If you let folks make you hate them, then you allow them to become a blessing blocker. That gives other people entirely too much power over your life.

Understand that no one can really block your blessings but you. It's true what the song says: "What God has for me, it is for me." For every door that a hater closes, God opens a door in another place. If somebody is digging a ditch for you to fall into, before you can fall in, Jesus will provide a bridge for you to walk across into a new blessing. Why people haven't figured this out yet, I don't know, but dissin' is wasted effort. Dissin' only blocks us from what we can receive.

That's why you need to tell the haters, crazy co-workers, and dysfunctional family members, "I am not going to let you or what you do block my blessing." Tell the devil that you know what he is up to. Speak boldly and tell him, "God's got something in the house for me!" So if someone hurts you or is hating on you, forgive that person, dismiss him or her, and go on in the house and join the party!

The Rest of The Story...

In the preceding chapters, we examined one of the greatest deliverance stories recorded in the Bible—the story of a fellow who struck out three times. In the judicial system, there is a saying: "Three strikes and you are out." On your third felony, you get much harsher sentences as a repeat offender. The Prodigal Son struck out three times. Strike one: he approached his father and said, "Dad, give me the portion of good that befalls me." So he was more concerned with money than he was about maintaining a relationship with his father. Strike two: he took the money, leaving him with a lot of money in his pocket but no sense in his head. Because of his foolishness, the money didn't stay in his pocket for very long. Strike three: because he had no employable skills and no money, when the economy went bad, he had to take a job trafficking an illegal substance: pig meat—because pigs were illegal.

The Prodigal Son made some tremendous, life-altering mistakes. But the good news is that the story doesn't end there. So we need to examine the rest of the story. To do this, let's look at Mark 5. There was an actual incident in the life of Jesus that inspired Him to tell the story of the Prodigal Son. In Mark 5, Jesus and His disciples arrived at the lake of Galilee near the region of Gerasene. As soon as Jesus got out of the boat, he was met by a man who had come out of the burial cave there. This man had an evil spirit in him and lived among the tombs. They couldn't keep him tied with chains anymore. Many times his hands and feet had been tied, but every time, he broke the chains and smashed the iron on his feet. He was too strong for anyone to control. Day and night he wandered among the tombs and through the hills, screaming and cutting himself with stones—self-inflicted pain. He was some distance away when he saw Jesus, so he ran and fell on his knees before Him and cried in a loud voice, "Jesus, son of the most high God, what do you want with me? For God's sake, I beg do not punish me." He said this because Jesus was saying, "Evil spirit, come out of this man." So Jesus asked him, "What is your name?" The man answered, "My name is Mob." There are so many of us named Mob. Like the Gerasene demoniac, the Prodigal Son was a miserable soul. He drifted away from his father; he put money over relationships, and he ended up a miserable soul. Any time you put anything over God, your life drifts into the abyss.

How miserable is he? Sometimes I want to call the story in Mark 5, "A Nude Dude in a Rude Mood," because that captured who the demoniac was. He was a miserable soul because of demon possession. He was more than manic; he was a demoniac—demon-possessed and psychotic. If he were alive today, he would be in a psychiatric ward for the criminally insane. He would have a room right next to Charles Manson.

It's not popular these days, but I'm still old-fashioned enough to believe in demon possession. Now you won't find the phrase "demon possession" at the local university library, and they won't be studying about it in medical school. However, the Bible affirms that demon possession is real. Now, there are some pseudo-scholars who will try to convince us that demons do not exist because they are students of science, and they believe in what is called empirical verification. This is the concept that says that if it can't be proven empirically and scientifically, then it is a non-reality; if it can't be verified using a test tube, a Bunsen burner, or a microscope, then it is not verifiable. Only that which can be proven through perception really exists.

So if you can't see it, touch it, taste it, or smell it, then it is a non-reality. But there are a whole lot of things that even a college professor must acknowledge as a reality but that cannot be seen. For example, ask a college professor, geologist, chemist, or botanist, "Do you believe in hope?" Most likely, they all will say, "Yes." Well, hope is a spirit. If you take an x-ray, you can't see hope in a person, but you can see the manifestation and the results of hope when it is in a person. We believe in fear because we all know that fear is real. But have you ever seen fear? No, you can't detect fear because fear is a spirit. What about self-destructive thinking? Yes, we know it exists, and we know its dangerous manifestations, but it cannot be seen as a tangible entity. All of these things are all spirits, so they cannot be seen. This is what the Bible is talking about; we simply have devised new names for old evils. Today, we call it psychosis and neurosis, but the Bible attributes these conditions to demons—evil spirits.

No one has ever seen electricity or can establish a concrete definition, but we see the end result in our lights and the other power-dependent devices we rely upon. No one has ever seen energy, but we all have seen the results of energy. Wherever you are sitting right now, there are television waves, radio waves, and microwaves all around you, producing sounds and images. You can't see them, but you can know they're there whenever you turn on a television or radio. When you warm something up in your microwave, you can't see them, but you know they're there because your food gets hot inside. Just like the images on television and radio, there are evil spirits. They become manifest when human beings give in to them and make them come alive in their personalities. Sometimes people will even bring evil spirits with them on the job.

Mark 5 tells us that this man was possessed by demons. But what are the characteristics of a demon-possessed person? A demon-possessed person is someone who is divided—psychologically bifurcated, perhaps trifurcated, or maybe even "polyfurcated," if you will. Verse 9 says, "For Jesus asked him, "What is your name?" The man answered, "My name is Mob." That word *mob* literally means *legions,* which is a garrison of 6,000 soldiers. He is saying, "I have so many demons in me that it's like there are 6,000 inside of me, tormenting me." The man had a mob of different temperaments, a mob of different mood swings, and a mob of different personality traits inside of him. So one minute he's feeling sad; then the next minute he's glad. One minute he's up; the next minute he's melancholy. How many mood swings does the average person go through in one day? How many mood swings can one person put together in just one hour? One of the characteristics of being demon-possessed is that the person is divided. One of the contributions Jesus makes to us is that Jesus has a way of harnessing all these divided energies that we have and bringing them into singleness of purpose.

Not only was the demoniac divided; he was defeated. He had a mob that was in control of him—his thoughts, his emotions, and even his actions. Have you ever felt like you lost your grip or that you're out of control? Being out of control means engaging in compulsive behavior or doing things that are self-destructive, like going after things you don't even like, or cutting yourself with stones. Have you ever asked yourself, "Why am I going in this direction because I know that it's hurting me?" You know that it's not good for you, but you go anyway.

This guy was defeated, divided, and demented. Many times his feet and hands had been tied, but every time, he broke the chains and smashed the iron on his feet. His strength could not be controlled. Day and night he wandered among the tombs of the graveyard and the hills, screaming and cutting himself. He was demented—screaming, restless, and naked. He was a dead man walking. Verse 2 says that as soon as Jesus got off the boat, He was met by a man that was living among the tombs. Now in the day of Jesus, the cemetery was a grotesque place where they discarded decayed bodies. He lived in tombstone territory, and he felt comfortable around dead folks. Now I know some messed-up folks, but I've never met anyone who was messed up enough to hang around a bunch of decayed dead bodies! He was a miserable soul, but by the power and might of the Savior, he doesn't stay that way. Where sin abounds, there grace does more abound. God's grace is always greater than any sin that any human being can commit. So no matter how great the sin, God's grace is always greater.

Here in the graveyard, a miserable soul meets a mighty Savior. Jesus had just come through a storm on the great Galilee, but when he got to tombstone territory, the demon-possessed man caught sight of Him. Immediately, the man got on his knees and started worshiping Jesus and begging the Messiah to leave him alone. That means the demons also made him schizophrenic. One minute he was worshiping God, and the next minute he was begging to be left alone. The disciples were frightened of him, and they stayed on the boat, but not Jesus—because He is a mighty Savior and is not intimidated nor put off by a demented soul. Whatever is over your head is under His feet. So the Savior got off the boat and started talking to the demons. He commanded, "Evil spirits, come out of this man."

Jesus is a mighty Savior; He has a great perception. This man was divided, demented, defeated, and dead. He was a nude dude in a rude mood, but in spite of how messed up he was, Jesus commanded the demons inside of him to come out. Despite the legion of demons that tormented the man, Jesus still saw him as a *man*, a human being (Mark 5:8). So many times we see people messed up, divided, demented, defeated, and dead, eating out of garbage cans, cracked out of their minds, and streaking up and down the street. We see gang bangers and hoochie mamas. We dehumanize them in our minds and think they are naughty by nature.

It's easier for us to deal with them when we make them less than human. But Jesus didn't call the demoniac a thug, a convict, or even a nutcase. Jesus never loses sight of the fact that regardless of how low a person may get, that one is still a human being made in the image of God. That's good news because no matter how low you get, Jesus has the discernment to see inside you to the beautiful creation that God made. This human tendency to dehumanize other people as objects enabled the institution of slavery to survive for 400 years. By declaring Black folks as less than human, slaveholders were able to commit their atrocities without feeling guilt or remorse. We love to dehumanize folk. Many people spend more money for their cats, dogs, and horses than they do on other human beings. Horses, dogs, and cats are not made in the image of God; humans are.

Jesus is a mighty Savior because He has perception, but also because He has power. I can perceive another person as a man or woman. I can see brothers and sisters on the street cracked out of their minds, selling their bodies in order to get another hit or fix. I can see that they are human beings because I'm seeing biblically, but I don't have any power to deal with their situation because I am not the Savior. Jesus, who is a mighty Savior, not only *perceives* who you are, but He has the *power* to get you back to where you need to be. He's got power. It's really interesting that everybody else tried to do something with this man but couldn't— not social services, not Narcotics Anonymous, and not Demons Anonymous. Getting an education couldn't do anything for him. Reform school was a waste of time. But when the mighty Savior met this miserable soul, Jesus looked at him and commanded, "Come out of this man, evil spirit."

Jesus has a way of speaking to the root of the problem. Jesus goes beyond all the superficialities and gets to the root of the problem—and the root of this man's problem was evil spirits. Jesus gets beyond the superficialities, beyond the analysis of the caseworker. He doesn't need to review the case file. The Bible says that the spirits came out; they had no choice but to obey Jesus' command.

There was a book written by Jack London entitled *The Call of the Wild*. It's a book about a ferocious, predatory wolf that was caught in a trap. The trapper had compassion for the wolf and nursed him back to health. Because of the trapper's kindness, the wolf that once had been violent and ferocious decided to stay next to the master. The wolf became domesticated. The wolf settled down his innate predatory impulses because of the kindness of this master. However, every night when the moon was out, he would hear the wolf pack from which he came. They would be howling, and the natural wolf instinct would rise up in him. He would hear what Jack London called "the call of the wild," or the call of the wolf pack trying to lure him back to the pack.

In his classic work, Jack London was not really writing about wolves. He was referring to human beings, for all of us have been in a trap and nursed back to health. We once were ferocious, but He calmed us down. Even when you are saved and calmed down, you can still hear the sound of the wolf pack. The wolf pack that God has divided you from is calling your name. Some people hear an alcohol wolf pack. Others hear the call of a whoring wolf pack. Many have been delivered from a toxic relationship that was a trick and a trap. Even though you are saved, even though you are sanctified, even though you are Holy Ghost-filled, even though you are biblically literate—every now and then you hear the call of the wolf pack, crying out to you, "Come back!" Were it not for the presence of the Master, many saints would have answered that call. That's a leash.

The demoniac became domesticated because he had the Master by his side. Jesus said, "Come out of this man, evil spirit." There is power in the voice of Jesus. Demons tremble at the name of Jesus! The demons said to the Master, "Jesus, don't kick us out of the territory. Let's us go into the pigs." Verse 11 says there was a large herd of pigs nearby, feeding on a hillside. Recall that the Prodigal Son was feeding the pigs and got lower than the pigs. Jesus let the evil spirits go out of the man and into the pigs. The passage says there were about 2,000 pigs, so each pig had three demons. Now with three demons in each pig, they began to do to the pigs what they were doing to the man. The Bible says that they rushed down the hill to the lake, and they were drowned. They knew they would rather be dead than live with demons tormenting them.

Some people are just like that; they would rather be dead than keep living like they are. They will say that they don't even want to live anymore. But notice that the passage says, "The men who had been taking care of the pigs ran to tell the news to the townspeople. People went to see what happened. When they went to see, verse 15 says that they saw that man who *used to have a* mob of demons in him. He was sitting calmly, clothed in his right mind. Before he met Jesus, he had been running, restless and demented. But since he met Jesus, for the first time in his life, he had peace on the inside. Only Jesus can give you your mind back. Only He can give you real peace. He will keep you in perfect peace if you keep your mind stayed on Him. He'll give you a mind, but the question is, "Where did the man get his clothes?"

The Bible says that everybody else went to town to tell what happened to the pigs and left the man that used to live in the cemetery by himself. Well, I believe that Jesus looked over in the boat at His disciples. Jesus probably looked at Andrew and said, "What size baseball cap is that?" Andrew answered, "Well, Jesus, it has an elastic ban in the back so it's flexible." Jesus said, "Well, let me have it." He took a hat from his disciples and put it on the naked man. He then looked at Peter and said, "Peter, do you have an extra throw-back jersey?" (Peter had a throwback jersey with a picture of Sampson on it.) Jesus said, "Let me have that throw-back jersey." He put the throwback jersey on the man. Then he looked at John, the beloved apostle, and said, "John, you got any extra Timberlands? Let me have those boots, Man! Let me have the caramel-colored ones." He took the shoes and placed them on the man's feet. Then He looked over at Judas and asked, "Do you have some FUBU?" Judas said, "What you mean? My FUBUs are too dirty." Jesus said, "Well, let me have your pants." Jesus gave the man his mind back, then looked through the church and gave him some clothes. By way of demonstration, Jesus was teaching that once He gets their minds right, He wants us to do what we can to get them a job, get them housing, get them solidly on the road to recovery.

Meanwhile, the swine investors saw that their pigs had gone down into the sea. The investors were the ones behind the pig cartel, for the real dealers are not the street brothers that get busted with a beeper. Let me digress briefly here. It's the brothers with the airplanes that bring the drugs into the country. I don't know any brothers in the hood that have planes. But the big boys saw what happened to all their illegal pig meat. When they saw what happened to the smoked sausage, the kilos of chitterlings, and the thousands of ounces of cracklings, they said, "Wait a minute, Jesus! That's 2,000 pigs! That's 8,000 pig feet!" Look at the big picture. When you see brothers on the street selling drugs, they are not the real dealers. The real dealers are the suppliers who have investments. If we get rid of illegal drug trafficking, it wouldn't just hurt the boys on the street because, to a certain degree, our economy is built around the sale of drugs and drug trafficking. If we get rid of drugs, it's going to hurt lawyers; we would have to lay off some police, and some corrections officers would have to go through the unemployment line.

There's a whole prison industry that has gotten rich because of illegal drugs in this country. One of the biggest and fastest-growing industries in America is that of building prisons. Somebody profits from getting the contract to build prisons. Somebody else profits from the contract for beds that go in the prison while another gets a contract for the sheets that go on the bed. With the money in their pockets from these huge contracts, they can then go around and buy commodities like cars because they've made money from supplying prisons with what is needed to incarcerate brothers and sisters. That means the car dealership gets money—all because the man who had the prison pillow contract got that contract simply because a brother got caught with some crackling. So that means Jesus came to town and set captives free and clothed them in their right mind, and then He took the crack and threw it into the river. In the church today, most of us can't deal with that kind of Jesus. The kind of Jesus many of us are comfortable with is the meek and lowly Jesus. We forget about the Jesus who overturned the tables of the moneychangers. Jesus is a radical, a militant, a revolutionary.

Jesus will get you in trouble if you truly follow Him. Jesus came to shake things up, and He did on that day. The Bible says they wanted Jesus to get out of town. So Jesus got in the boat and started going out. But when the man looked at where he was and looked at the investor who wanted to lure him back to what he had been in—when he looked at the investors and the hog meat that was drowning in the water and looked at Jesus who was leaving— the Bible said that he ran and tried to get in the boat to go with Jesus. That's understandable because having been that messed up, he would naturally want to hang out with Jesus all of the time. That's what should happen when Jesus delivers us—we should want to hang out with Him all the time. The man was probably saying, "I've got to go with you because can't nobody do me like Jesus!" But Jesus said, "No. I don't want you to go with me. I've got a better assignment for you. I want you to go back home, and I want you to show folks what I have done for you. I want you to just tell somebody about how messed up you were until you met up with a miracle. Tell them, 'I was demented. I was defeated. I was divided and I was dead, but Jesus came by and spoke to my demons. And after He finished speaking to my demons, I was sitting clothed in my right mind.'"

There are people in the world like this man and like the Prodigal Son. They've got a testimony—a powerful testimony that can change somebody's life. When you have been all messed up and divided, but Jesus delivers you from your demons, you ought to go tell it. There's somebody who needs to know that no matter how far out there you get, no matter how far into the far country that you get, when you meet Jesus, He'll put you back into your right mind. Jesus says that no matter how low you are, he still sees you as a human being, a creation of the Father. Like the Prodigal Son and his father, you can't do anything to make your heavenly Father disregard your worth. Like the demoniac, you cannot get so consumed by demons that God no longer regards your humanity. Even in the most messed-up human being, He sees someone who is made in His image.

There is a well-known story about a minister who held up a $20 bill to his congregation and asked, "How many of you would want to have this $20 bill?" Of course, all hands in the congregation went up. The minister then crumpled the bill in his hand and asked the question again. All hands in the congregation went up a second time. Finally, the minister let the bill fall to the floor and stepped on it, grinding it into the floor until it was dirty. "Now," he asked, "how many of you still would want this bill?" Every hand in the congregation was raised for a third time. "We all can learn a valuable lesson from this," the minister said. "No matter what I did to the $20 bill, you still wanted it because it did not decrease in value. That's the way God looks at us. There is nothing we can do that will diminish our value in His eyes."

Here's an important part about God's deliverance. God doesn't just save you to be cute or satisfied with yourself. God doesn't rescue you just so that you can be important. God didn't just rescue you so that you can be a part of the do-nothing committee. God saved you from your mess because He has a contract with you. And the contract is this: "If I deliver you, you will tell somebody what I've done for you. If you look back over your life and see where I've brought you from, then you've got to tell somebody." He expects you to tell somebody, "The reason that I know He's real is because He wouldn't have brought me this far"— when the devil should have killed you while he had you, but you lived to see another day.

That's the rest of the story. You can always come back home to the Father. When you meet up with Him, He'll clothe you in your right mind—the mind of Christ. He'll pick you up out of the tombs and wipe away the demons that once haunted you and tormented you. He will pull you out of the graveyard. Some people are so consumed by their demons that they are living dead. They are alive, but because of alcoholism, because of drug addiction, because of sexual addictions, or an addiction to lies, drama, character assassinations, and so forth, they are of no earthly good to the Kingdom of God. They simply wander around in torture, just like the demoniac.

The Prodigal Son had it good until he messed up, but then he came back. The demoniac never knew what it was to have the good life until he met Jesus. Either way, Jesus can do it for you. Whether you've gone to the far country and landed in the hog pen, or whether you've been tormented all of your life, He can and will fix it for you.

Epilogue:
Pass it On!

Once, after I had blessed some babies at St. Stephen, a parishioner approached me and said, "Pastor, that was a moving and memorable experience. But what I want to know is how much of that ceremony do you think those babies will remember when they are all grown up?" That was a good question, because two of the babies were sound asleep, and one was crying. But even if they had been paying attention, those babies were not conscious that hands were being laid on them in consecration and dedication.

We can expand that question to ask, "What will our children remember about life under our roof when they're all grown up?" I remember when I was baptized, and how, afterwards, my parents took me out to dinner. It was so special for me and left an impression upon my life. Every person remembers some things about what happened while growing up—but what? Will they remember a praying mother? Will they remember a father with faith, wisdom, and compassion? Will they remember the times that the family prayed together? Or will they remember an absentee daddy? A deadbeat dad? Will they remember an alcoholic mom? An abusive mother? Those memories, whatever they are, will stick with them even after they're all grown up.

Part of the reason why the Prodigal Son had enough sense to go home from the hog pen was because he remembered he had a good home to go back to. That means some of what his father had taught and lived had rubbed off on him and left an indelible impression in his mind and on his heart. He had enough of his father's love in him that, even though he squandered his inheritance and was living in a wild and crazy hog pen, he knew that it was peaceful and pleasant at his father's house. He remembered his identity. Sitting in that hog pen, he must have asked himself, "Who's your daddy? You have no business sitting in this hog pen, competing with the hogs just to get a taste of slop!" So how do we raise our children so that, even if they have a prodigal stage of life, they retain deep within the recesses of their hearts and minds the spiritual teachings that will serve them for a lifetime?

Adults remember what really happened to them as children. They can't remember that their parents loved them if it didn't happen. They won't remember being valued at home if it didn't happen. They will only remember what happened. So a wise parent is one who is trying to give his or her children something to remember when they grow up. Hopefully, they'll be able to say things like, "Boy, I remember what Dad said about praying when you're in trouble."

Now, it can be argued that memories are only memories. After all, you can't buy a car with a memory. No one has ever purchased a house or put food on the table with memories. So why does it matter what you remember? It matters a lot because when the past passes, it does more than just pass. All of us are the products of our past, and some of us today are suffering from memories of a dysfunctional and tormented past. The past colors and shapes our perceptions. What goes into a girl will come out in the woman. What goes into the boy will come out in the man. What goes into the child will come out in the adult. We are products of our past. That's why there's a whole school of psychology called transactional analysis, which says if you want to understand why adults act the way they do, you must look into their childhood.

It's like the story of the pike fish that was put in an aquarium. They put a glass shield in the aquarium, and on the other side of the glass shield they put minnows. When the pike saw the minnows, he said, "I've got to get some of those minnows." When the pike started charging toward the minnows, he bumped his head. They kept that transparency in the aquarium for a month before removing it. From that point on, even though there were minnows all around the pike and no glass barrier protected them, the pike never tried to attack them. The pike had been conditioned, because of his past experiences, to believe that if there were minnows around, he could not have them.

Many people are just like that pike. They grew up with invisible barriers that made them believe certain things were unavailable to them—love, peace, healthy relationships, financial well-being, or spiritual grounding. Even though the invisible barrier has been removed from their circumstances, they still have a barrier in their minds. We talk about a glass ceiling, which is a real phenomenon. But sometimes the glass or the barrier exists only in your mind. God has surrounded you with minnows—blessings and opportunities—that you can't see because of your past conditioning. You may be limited and inhibited because of your past. But our past can be either beneficial or detrimental to us in adulthood.

In 2 Timothy 1:5, we read about four generations of Christians. Paul, who writes this epistle to Timothy, said, "I have been reminded of your sincere faith, which first lived in your grandmother Lois" (NIV). And Lois was one of Paul's converts. So Lois caught the spiritual bug from Paul. But then he goes on to say, "And in your mother Eunice...." So Lois caught it from Paul, and then daughter Eunice caught it from her mother Lois. And what they both caught was now living in Timothy. That was spiritual DNA passed down generationally from Paul to Lois, to Eunice, and then on to Timothy. How do we transmit faith from one generation to another? How do we pass on to our children the faith that we inherited from our parents?

Unlike the Prodigal Son, Timothy apparently had no period of sowing his oats or exploring the world. Timothy began serving the Lord at a young age. He was doing the Lord's work, but he was having some hard times. He was pastoring a church in Ephesus, a difficult place to lead Christians because the Ephesians had their own god—the goddess Diana, and there was an amphitheater there in her honor. In addition to seeing his protégée in a tough ministry assignment, his mentor knew he did not have much longer to live. Young Timothy did not want to imagine a world without the apostle Paul. On top of that, the emperor Nero, Christianity's chief antagonist, was vehement in his persecution of those who followed the Way. All these pressures were mounting against Timothy—low self-esteem, a difficult pastorate in Ephesus, the threat of persecution from the Roman government, and the impending execution of his spiritual father.

Timothy was totally discouraged and wanted to quit. Paul wrote to Timothy to encourage him by reminding him of his rich spiritual heritage. He wanted Timothy to strengthen himself, drawing from the well of his memories of faith that he inherited from his mother Eunice and his grandmother Lois. Actually, it's a miracle that Timothy was a Christian in the first place because Timothy grew up in south Galatia. According to Acts 16:1-2 (NIV), Paul "came to Derbe and then to Lystra, where a disciple named Timothy lived, whose mother was a Jewess and a believer, but whose father was a Greek." Derbe and Lystra were located in south Galatia, which was the equivalent of today's South Central Los Angeles. Nothing expresses the hard-core nature of urban living better than South Central. There are countless gangs—Black gangs, Puerto Rican gangs, Cuban gangs, other Hispanic gangs, and European gangs. It is estimated that there are over 80,000 gang members in Compton and South Central. In Paul's day, Galatia was the worst place to be. So Timothy grew up in a rough area with a heathen father. But he had a praying, believing mother. There are many households today like the one Timothy grew up in—Mama was a faithful churchgoer, but Daddy was an unbeliever. But despite growing up in the worst conditions and having a father who did not believe, Timothy inherited a strong faith from his mother and grandmother.

In 2 Timothy 3:14-15, Paul urged, "But as for you, continue in what you have learned and have become convinced of, because you know those from whom you learned it, and how from infancy you have known the holy Scriptures, which are able to make you wise for salvation through faith in Christ Jesus" (NIV). From infancy, someone had taught Timothy the Word. When he became an adult, he was able to remember those teachings.

Timothy didn't gain spiritual knowledge from a gang or from his Greek father. It came from his mother and grandmother. What his mother had gotten from her mother she passed on to Timothy. She passed on to him a legacy of faith that got him over in Ephesus. At his lowest moment, in his toughest time, he was able to remember the faith that his mother had given to him, and that gave him the power to deal with the perplexities that were plaguing his life.

It is important that parents, mothers and fathers alike, pass on their faith to their children who can only remember what they have gotten. You can pass on a whole lot to your children—such as a passion for material things, like Sean Jean, FUBU, and Xbox. When your children are grown and facing difficult situations like Timothy did, Air Jordans won't get them through. Reebok can't help them. Tommy Hilfiger has nothing to give. But if they have love and respect for God in their hearts, if they have faith, a tradition and a legacy of faith that has been passed on to them by their parents, they will be able to make it through the difficult times. And since human beings can remember only what they see and experience, your children won't remember to pray if they didn't see you praying. They won't remember to forgive if you never forgave anyone. They won't remember to praise God if they never saw you praise Him.

That's why wise parents pass on their faith to their children in the developmental years. Timothy's mother began when he was an infant. She didn't wait until he was a troubled teenager in and out of juvenile hall. It's too late then. You can't afford to wait until the world has conditioned them to be everything but faithful and then try to tell them, "Oh, by the way, before you leave home, I need to tell you what faith can do." This has to happen when they are very young.

It's important that parents teach children about faith themselves. This is a responsibility that God has given to parents, not to the church. The church is not a babysitter. Children's choirs and youth ministries are not babysitters. Parents have a responsibility to bring their children to church, not send them. Children need to see and hear their parents say "Amen!" They need to see them worship, for they won't remember it if they don't see it for themselves. In fact, as children grow up, parents need to be telling them bedtime stories about David and how he fought Goliath, for when they are grown up, they are going to have some Goliaths. They can't possibly know that they can defeat Goliath if they didn't experience their parent's doing it. Parents need to teach their children, by precept and example, how they can survive in the heat of troubling times. When they know that God will make a way, they won't run to the dope man, and they won't drown in their sorrows, telling their troubles to Johnny Walker. They will have faith.

What better tribute to good parenting than to hear an adult say, "I remember what Momma always told me about the importance of prayer," or "My Daddy taught me to trust in the Lord." But that's hard for some parents because some are timid and insecure about witnessing to their children. That's why they pay the preacher to witness to their children. But no preacher can do what God wants and expects parents to do. Parents are supposed to train their children and bring them up in the way they should go. God didn't tell the church to do that. He didn't command the pastor or the youth minister to teach other folks' children about the way that they should go.

Parents must teach their children, just like the father taught the Prodigal Son and his brother. He had to have taught them all along, but he also taught them as young adult men. He taught the Prodigal Son and his brother a valuable lesson in forgiveness. Some parents have taught their children very little. Some children have no idea how their parents pay bills. When you buy that new television or go to the grocery store, you need to tell your children, "The only reason we're going to be able to afford this is because God is making a way." They need to know where things come from—On High! Tell your children about how God makes a way in hard times. Tell them how He made a way during your hard times. Tell them how God paid the bills. Tell your children how nobody got sick even when you lost your job and your health benefits. That way, when they get older, they'll remember whom to turn to when life gets rough. The Prodigal Son knew to go to his father. Your children need to know that they can go to the Father, and He is always ready to receive them with rejoicing.

I thank God for my own mother. She died when I was a boy, but she still told me about God in the few years we had together. She told me about Jesus. After she died and after I got a little older and started living in *Galatia*, with my own trials and tribulations, I didn't have to drink or do drugs because I had something to draw on. I made it over my difficult times because I was able to draw back on something my mother told me. She said, "Son, if you pray, God answers prayer. If you trust Him and never doubt, He will surely bring you out." I didn't want to hear it when I was a little kid, but those are beautiful words to me now. I didn't understand it when I was an adolescent, but I thank God that I heard her words so that when the time came, I could draw back on it. It has been during the difficult times that I reminded myself, "Wait a minute. Momma said 'God will take care of you. Be not dismayed, whatever betide; God will take care of you.'" On the strength of her words, one day I tried God for myself, and I'm a witness that He will take care of you.

One of the biggest problems with parents today is most of them are more concerned about being a friend to their children than about being a parent. Friends try to compromise, call a truce, or negotiate a treaty. Parents make tough calls and unpopular decisions, like making you go to church when you thought you were grown enough to stay at home and sleep late. More parents need to know who their children are hanging out with and say, "Oh no! You're not going to mess with this child....You're not bringing him into my house....You're not going out with those girls." They'll be upset at first, but one day they'll be grateful and shout "Hallelujah!"

Most people who are able to accomplish anything at all in life have done so because somebody prayed for them. Somebody prayed, "Lord, let me live long enough to see my children live to become adults." But if they died before the prayer was answered, they had a contingency: "Lord, if I can't live to see them become adults, then please take care of my children."

So what are you teaching your children? What are you passing on to your children? They know enough about DMX and L'il Kim. They need to know more about Jesus. They need to know about the God who's a way-maker, a bill-payer, a heavy-load sharer, and a bridge over troubled water. They need to know about a God who is able to do exceedingly, abundantly above all that we can ask or imagine. They need to know about a God who is able to open up a door. They need to know about a God who's able to make giants come down. They need to know about a God who can open up a door where there is no door. They need to know about a God that is a miracle worker. And they won't know it if you don't tell them. And let me tell you that the God my mama talked about is real, yes He is.

Now that you know all of these things, answer the question: *Who's Your Daddy?*

About The Author

Kevin W. Cosby, D. Min.

A staunch proponent of education, Dr. Cosby earned a Bachelor's degree from Eastern Kentucky University in Richmond, a Master of Divinity degree from The Southern Baptist Theological Seminary in Louisville, and a Doctor of Ministry degree from United Theological Seminary in Dayton, Ohio. He has been awarded honorary doctorates from Eastern Kentucky University, Bellarmine University, and Campbellsville University.

Dr. Cosby has held administrative and teaching assignments at Kentucky State University, the University of Louisville, The Southern Baptist Theological Seminary, and United Theological Seminary. His exceptional oratory skills have produced lecture engagements at universities and institutions around the world, including Harvard University. His local community service includes boards of trustees for both Kentucky State University and the University of Louisville.

St. Stephen Baptist Church

Since 1979, the Reverend Dr. Kevin W. Cosby has served as Senior Pastor of St. Stephen Baptist Church in Louisville, Kentucky. Due greatly to his practical and dynamic Bible teachings, the congregation has grown from 500 to approximately 14,000 members with three large beautifully appointed campuses: a 1,000-seat church in Louisville, and 500-seat churches in Jeffersonville, Indiana and Radcliff, Kentucky. The church conducts mid-week Bible studies and multiple services on Saturdays and Sundays to accommodate the crowds. It also broadcasts its full worship services weekly at www.ssclive.tv.

In 2010 *Outreach* magazine recognized St. Stephen as one of the 100 largest churches in America, and *Emerge* magazine identified it as one of six "super churches" of the South. St. Stephen has the largest Christian African American education program in Kentucky and sponsors development of the full person, through education, science, art, music, and culture. Annually it awards $50,000 in college scholarships.

Under Dr. Cosby's vision, St. Stephen has grown to become the largest private Black employer in Kentucky and has led the city's economic investment in one of the poorest neighborhoods in the nation. Dr. Cosby's leadership brings Blacks and whites together to channel social and economic capital into poor neighborhoods. Dr. Cosby promotes Black entrepreneurship, hard work, self-reliance, accountability, and ethical wealth building. St. Stephen leads by example. A debt-free institution controlled by Blacks, its $23 million in assets include more contiguous property than any other Black private institution in West Louisville.

St. Stephen is dedicated to service and to justice. It speaks up for the poor, promotes voter registration drives, conducts health clinics, and provides transportation for seniors. At no cost to the city, it renovated the nearby California Community Center, and It established and built a Family Life Center, which includes a state-of-the-art indoor fitness center, racquet ball court, basketball court, an indoor walking/running track, an upscale women's clothing boutique, a sit-down family restaurant, youth after school and summer enrichment programs, and addiction recovery meetings. It also has provided facilities for West Louisville's only physical therapy rehabilitation center. More information on this visionary church is found at www.ssclive.org.

SIMMONS COLLEGE OF KENTUCKY INC.

While St. Stephen Baptist Church is Dr. Cosby's first calling, Simmons College of Kentucky Inc. has become his mission outreach project. From 1879 to 1930, Simmons College was a national leader in higher education for African Americans. Established by formerly enslaved Kentucky Baptists, Simmons became a full university with a law school and a medical school. But during the Great Depression, its campuses suffered foreclosure, and as its programs were scaled back, it became a small Bible college in a remote part of the city's poorest area.

In 1997, Dr. Cosby led his church to purchase the nearby four-acres of the former Simmons campus, even though at the time, he was unsure of how the property would be used. He prayed in his heart that God would allow him to reclaim the mission of this historically Black institution of higher learning, even though, at the time, it seemed like a pipe dream. Yet in 2005 Dr. Kevin Cosby became the 13th president of Simmons and promptly began reclaiming the college's original mission of offering a full curriculum for impoverished African American youth.

In the last 12 years, Dr. Cosby has refused nearly $1,000,000 in compensation that would otherwise be due to someone of his stature in order to assure the college's economic stability and build a comprehensive curriculum. Simmons' priority is students, maintaining a small faculty-student ratio, and it embraces entrepreneurial education. Under Dr. Cosby's visionary leadership, Simmons gained accreditation by the Association of Biblical Higher Education (ABHE). In 2015 the U.S. Department of Education granted Simmons status as the nation's 107th Historically Black College and University (HBCU). Enrolling over 200 students,

Simmons offers baccalaureate and associate degrees in business, cross-cultural communications, music, religious studies, and sociology—all designed to strengthen the five institutions so critical to the African American community: churches, families, schools, businesses, and media. In the last two years, Simmons has graduated 55 students, all of whom have completed college with zero debt.

Simmons has recently become the headquarters for the National Baptist Convention of America International Inc. (NBCA). An organization first formed in 1880, this voluntary convention of African American Baptists has over 3.5 million constituents. This will be a beneficial relationship for the college, the convention, and the city. The NBCA has already purchased a beautiful 56-acre retreat/conference center in southwestern Louisville, and its annual sessions will bring attention to Simmons and tourism to the city, while Simmons' program in religious studies and its community leadership programs will support the mission of the convention.

Simmons College and the NBCA along with the Progressive Baptist Convention Inc., and the Cooperative Baptist Fellowship have partnered together to sponsor a three-year comprehensive religious and community education program that creates awareness of our individual and collective responsibility to do God's work of economic justice—leading up to the 400th anniversary of slavery in America. Known as the Angela Project in honor of the first Christian enslaved woman to step foot on American soil in 1619, the program will bring leaders together to advocate for Black communities and institutions in places of power, challenge businesses and churches to invest in Black neighborhoods, while teaching Black communities to better use their economic resources.

PUBLICATIONS

Dr. Cosby has authored five highly-acclaimed books: *Get Off Your But!: Messages, Musings & Ministries to Empower the*

African-American Church; As They Went; Treasure Worth Seeking; Who's Your Daddy?: Life Lessons from the Prodigal Son, and *Be Loyal to the Royal*. He has been a contributing writer to a number of books, journals, and newspapers.

Personal and Contact Information

Dr. Kevin Cosby has been the subject of many national articles and documentaries, which consistently list him among the most influential leaders in the Commonwealth of Kentucky. His 2007 selection as "Louisvillian of the Year" is a tribute to his outstanding contributions to the community. Louisville Magazine ranked him #1 of the Top Ten Religious Leaders in Louisville. In the spring of 2012, he was inducted into the Hall of Distinguished Alumni at Eastern Kentucky University. Although Dr. Cosby has achieved many notable accomplishments, he is most known for his intense commitment to serving God through improving the lives of others.

Dr. Cosby is married to the former Barnetta Turner. They are the parents of two adult children and one beautiful granddaughter.

To contact Dr. Cosby for more information regarding his ministries and community leadership activities or for speaking engagements, email seniorpastor@ssclive.org or phone: 502-583-6798. More information may be found at http://www.drkevincosby.com.

| WHO'S YOUR DADDY? | *Other Books*
by Kevin W. Cosby, D. Min. |

As They Went...

Dr. Cosby examines the testimonies of God's faithful followers who experienced His blessings, mercy, and grace because they chose the route of obedience to God. In his sermons and writings, Dr. Cosby presents well-known Bible stories in a fresh way. After reading this book, you will understand Enoch, Abraham, Moses, Peter, Philip, and others in a new way that is relevant to your own life. This book is not the same old clichés about obeying worn-out platitudes, but about empowering people as they answer the call of God.

Be Loyal to the Royal in You

Previously published as Treasure Worth Seeking, Dr. Cosby examines five ways that believers benefit from being a royal priesthood—in wisdom, truth, guidance, power, and joy. Being a royal is not just an abstract pious status you attain, but an understanding your divine heritage that enables you to attain excellence in all areas of your life

GET OFF YOUR BUT!

In this new paradigm for the proclamation of the Gospel, Dr. Cosby examines twelve challenges that face all communities. He not only gives inspiring biblical examples of meeting those challenges, but also outlines practical ways that churches can make a difference in the lives of those they serve. While set in the context of the African American church, this book speaks to all churches that want to show the love of Christ to people in a real way. When you read this book, your life will be better, your community will be stronger, and your church will be more relevant. But first, you must get off your but!

JESUS GREW, SO HOW ABOUT YOU?

This book looks at Jesus' life, both the recorded and hidden parts, to glean important lessons about personal growth. Christians say they want to be like Jesus, but they overlook the clues in Scripture about how growth truly occurs. The majority of Jesus' life and preparation went unrecorded, hidden from our eyes. Growth toward maturity takes much time, humility, and discipline and is unseen by others before we can make a public show. Centered on Luke 2:52, Dr. Cosby shows readers how personal growth must include all areas of our lives: physical, educational, spiritual, and social.

WHO'S YOUR DADDY?

Using vivid imagery and true-to-life situations, Dr. Cosby offers hope that every person can be united with their heavenly Father in a healthy relationship. Dr. Cosby explores how the Prodigal Son's experience mirrors the life cycle of every individual's relationship with God. Within the context of the African American male, Dr. Cosby shows how cultivating a relationship with God can heal the wounds of our absent or imperfect fathers and can enable us to have better relationships in all areas of our lives. Reading this book will forever transform the way you view the story of the prodigal son.

Most titles available at the St. Stephen Baptist Church bookstore, Simmons College of Kentucky bookstore, other Christian bookstores ,and Amazon.com. E-book editions available at www.drkevincosby.com.

www.ingramcontent.com/pod-product-compliance
Lightning Source LLC
Chambersburg PA
CBHW071904020426
42331CB00010B/2657